'FOWLNESS'
The Mystery Isle
1914-1939

'Fowlness'
has been published
as a Limited Edition
of which this is

Number

A list of original
subscribers is printed
at the back
of this book

The windmill.

'FOWLNESS'
The Mystery Isle
1914-1939

BY

JOHN S. DOBSON

BARON
MCMXCVI

PUBLISHED BY BARON BIRCH FOR QUOTES LIMITED
AND PRODUCED BY KEY COMPOSITION,
SOUTH MIDLANDS LITHOPLATES,
CHENEY & SONS, HILLMAN PRINTERS (FROME) LIMITED
AND WBC BOOK MANUFACTURERS

ISBN 0 86023 565 3

CONTENTS

ACKNOWLEDGEMENTS

I am grateful to Major A. S. Hill (retired), Shoebury Garrison Archives, who supplied invaluable documents and photographs relating to the construction of the road and bridge to Foulness; Burnham-on-Crouch residents, Bob Cole and the late Mr J. Chittick; the late George Clark, former Editor of the *Burnham and Dengie Hundred Advertiser*, and Jim Worsdale, former Editor of the *Evening Echo*, who not only previewed the manuscript, but kindly offered to proof read the work. For that and his encouragement, I am duly grateful.

To Mrs B. Dent, née Belton, the late Mrs P. Belton, Leon Dobson, Fred Boniface, Bob Crump and all those who donated or lent photographs of the island and for refreshing my memory, and to Pat Thorn, for typing the final draft copy for the publisher, my grateful thanks.

Finally, of course, I must thank my family, especially my wife, who has patiently endured many hours of my frustration in trying to master modern technology, and Pauline and Terry Dean, Dr Susan Dobson and Dr Clive Griffen, who helped an 80-year-old computer illiterate to use a word processor. Without their help it is doubtful that it would have been completed.

BIBLIOGRAPHY AND SOURCES

The Shoe 1982 by Major A. Hill RA ret'd
The Roadmakers of Foulness by Jack Taylor 1920/22
The History of the Road to Foulness by Pat Arnold
The History of the Rochford Hundred 1867 by Philip Benton
Foulness Island Primary School, A History 1846-1988 R. W. Crump
The Evening Echo
Foulness Archaeology Society
The John Lilley Photo Collection
Burnham on Crouch and District, Local History and Amenity Society

FOREWORD by Jim Worsdale

I was born, raised and educated in the town of Southend-on-Sea, perhaps half a dozen miles from the guarded gateway to Foulness. The Island might well have been on the moon, for all I knew about it. A lifetime later, little has changed: Foulness remains, to outsiders, a remote and mysterious place.

Though fast-approaching my half-century as a journalist, much of it spent locally with newspapers that have reported sketchily and occasionally about Foulness and its people, I have visited the island only a few times; then, merely to see events or people I was allowed to see, by official pre-arrangement. No wonder it was dubbed the isle of secrets, even though senior military types resent the label and deny its implications.

Foulness is, though, known to relatively few. It is known *of* because of the weapon testing grounds, the tragedies it suffered in the East Coast floods of 1953 and the controversy that raged through the late 1960s and into the next decade over the possible siting on the adjacent Maplin Sands of London's proposed third international airport. When that project was killed off by the Government, Foulness faded into obscurity like the island and the sands, when dense North Sea fog suddenly and terrifyingly descends.

Now at last, we can know much more *about* Foulness, thanks to John Dobson. He writes from the heart, as a man who grew up there, went to school there, worked there, made many friends there and lives now, with the island on the horizon as he looks from the windows of his home on the nearby mainland.

He has not produced some erudite tome, some dry, date-filled historical record. Rather, his is a personal story of a place where time long seemed to stand still, before moving slowly and inexorably on; a fascinating account of a rare little corner of England where, even now, much remains unchanged from long ago.

John Dobson served his community and his fellows for many years as a local councillor and magistrate. Now, in retirement, he does another fine service in setting down much that would otherwise have been sadly lost.

7

The island from the 1920 OS map.

INTRODUCTION

To the best of my ability this is a social history of a period in the life of a unique Island, a nostalgic account of a now vanished way of life. Foulness is like no other island in the United Kingdom, yet it is only approximately 50 miles from London. For centuries it was isolated from the mainland by rivers and the North Sea. Apart from a brief period after construction of the road and bridge to the mainland, before the Ministry of Defence restricted entry to the public, the isolation has remained. The island remains a mystery to most people.

I have often thought that someone should attempt to record the way of life on the island from 1914 to 1939, an eventful era in its history, in many ways truly remarkable. With many of my contemporaries gone, it has become a matter of urgency to put down the memories that would otherwise be lost forever.

I refer to a period of immense change, during a steady decline in the island's population, which today leaves it without a school, no resident parson, district nurse or village policeman. The Government agent no longer resides there. These people were the very life blood of village life.

As a member of the Dobson family, who arrived on the island in 1841, I feel privileged to have lived my first twenty-five years there from 1914. The memories come flooding back.

DEDICATION

To my Grandmother, Mary Ann Dobson, 1850-1937,
a wonderful lady.

9

The first view of the island when landing at the Quay from the River Roach, taken in 1996, which is at it was in the 1920s.

PROLOGUE

There is no record to say when Foulness became an island, but research by the AWE (Foulness) Archaeological Society suggests Foulness was occupied for a short period circa 180-280 AD. Pottery relating to that period was found at Lt Shelford in the 1970s. Foulness is the largest of a group of six islands in the Thames Estuary, including Potton, Rushley, Havengore, New England and Wallasea. New England, adjacent to and now part of Foulness was, in the 17th century, part-owned by St Bartholomew's and a house belonging to the hospital stood on the island, but there are no records of its use.

During the Roman occupation, Foulness was situated between the military settlements of Bradwell *Othena* on the Dengie peninsula and *Reculver* across the Thames estuary. The sea wall was probably constructed in the 12th century; so began the reclamation of Foulness island and, after seven stages of that reclamation, the area is nearly 7,000 acres today. It was recorded that in 1049, in the reign of Edward the Confessor, several vessels landed there.

The population of the island in the middle ages consisted of a few shepherds, but increased rapidly with the arrival of arable farming and in 1801 the population was 396; by 1871 it had risen to 754. With the increased population, water supplies, which had previously been imported, became a problem, so the first wells were sunk in 1830 and eventually further wells were sunk to a depth of 500ft at several farms.

Foulness was originally part of a group of Parishes — Rochford, Sutton, Little Wakering, Shopland and Little Stambridge. In 1546 Foulness was declared a separate parish and the original wooden church of St Mary the Virgin was erected. It was eventually demolished in 1846, as it was considered too small for the growing population. The present church was dedicated in 1852.

The ancient road to Foulness was known as the 'Broomway', as the route across the sands was marked by placing brooms at intervals. The practice was common in the 15th century and was recorded in 1419 by one William Daunger, a bailiff of Great Wakering, as an accepted feature of the district.

The rich arable land was widely sought after and the records show that the Crown granted Hubert de Burgh the Manor of Foulness and, after his son, it passed on to Guy de Rochford. Sir Guy died in 1274 and then it passed to the Bohun family. He was followed by Lord Rich in 1546 and, after the death of Charles Rich, the estate was eventually split up and in 1678 passed to Daniel Finch. The Manor remained in the Finch family until it was sold to the Government in 1915.

In 1849 an artillery range was established at Shoeburyness for the use of Woolwich Arsenal, as the Woolwich range could not cope with the new guns then on trial. However, in 1862, there were complaints by fishermen and bargees regarding several near misses and in 1882, as the range of guns increased, a Bill was passed closing the foreshore.

Then followed a long legal battle between the War Office and John Emerson, the Lord of Great Wakering Manor. In 1891 the Law Lords ruled in John Emerson's favour, forcing the War Office to buy up more foreshore. In 1904 Rev J. Brown, Rector of Foulness, wrote to the Secretary of State regarding the danger to the public from shellfire. The letter was acknowledged, but no action was taken.

More pressure followed and an enquiry was held in October 1911. The result was a proposal that a road should be built between Great Wakering and Great Shelford, Foulness. On 28 June 1914 a shot was fired in Sarajevo (Serbia) and the nation was at war. With its now bottomless purse the War Office grasped the opportunity to link the island with the mainland. The old Broomway road from Great Wakering to Foulness, apart from being a treacherous route across the sands, had always posed maintenance problems. In fact, in the early 18th century it was closed for a period, but was eventually opened on the understanding that Great Wakering was to be responsible for keeping it open, the cost supplemented by donations from Squire Finch and the Parish rate.

During the 19th century the Church of England school was erected in 1846 to hold 120 pupils, for in 1841 the population had risen to 674; 437 males and 237 females. By 1871 the population comprised 447 males and 307 females. The first master was Clement Cater.

The School Log commences on 13 December 1872 and records local problems in the school's history; 'but few children attended during the week owing to heavy rain making the roads very bad'. The journey to school was always a problem, for many of the children travelled across treacherous plank bridges, which on occasions were under water.

Facilities in the school were basic and the log book reports the open fires were hardly adequate. Parents were expected to pay for education and it was 2d for the eldest child and a penny for the rest. On 20 May 1881 the log book reveals the average attendance was 58 and nearly all the older boys, some as young as seven years old, were away at work, earning 3d a week, a sufficient inducement to keep any child away from school.

The Board of School Governors realised that attendances were a never-ending problem and, although attendance officers had been appointed, they seemed to have missed Foulness. Then in 1884 an attendance officer appeared on the island. The effect was dramatic and attendance went up to 100% for the first time. Parents, however, were disgruntled, for they missed the 3d per week. As for the children, many had not been to school for years, were backward, and found themselves in the infant classes.

In 1872, Mr William Wilkinson was appointed Headmaster and Mrs Wilkinson, Headmistress. He was extremely enthusiastic, but he found the children sadly lacking in education and he reported on a plan of campaign to improve the standards. In February 1874 he recorded 'plan of notation succeeded'. The subjects being taught were geometry, reading, writing, needlework and algebra, scripture being taught by the Rector.

In 1872 a letter was sent to Rev Dalton of the school governors from the Education Department in Whitehall, informing him that, as the school had been enlarged, there was no further need for a separate school at Courtsend.

After some interruption, the school was reopened in November 1874 and the Wilkinsons continued to teach there until 1891. The annual report of HM Inspector commented that he could not report any improvement, that there was a general shortcoming and that the law was being openly violated; detailed work of the infants was unsatisfactory.

The new term started in October 1891 and a Mr George Leeds and his wife were appointed as Headmaster and Headmistress. In 1894 they were joined by Miss Maggie Whent from Nazewick to work as a pupil teacher, but sadly Miss Whent died of typhoid fever in 1895.

While many children had long and lonely walks to school, none compared with the Peg's family, whose address was HM Coastguard ship the *Frolic*, on which their father was a serving officer.

Chemical lavatories for both sexes were the norm and in 1905 an additional fireplace was installed, but in January 1907 it was reported the heating system was inadequate, when the temperature fell as low as 32F. School holidays, and particularly the summer holiday, depended on the harvest period, for often the older boys were late returning to school.

In the 20th century, attendances were at an all-time high and in 1908 and for subsequent years, the school won the Rochford Hundred award for attendances. The enforcement officers no doubt contributed to this success, but Headmasters with a strict code of conduct had a lot do to with it.

The log book is revealing; November 1913 'took all the children to Newlands to see the Sopwith plane, where it had landed. It was seen to take off, but landed in the next field'. In 1914 War came and its effect on school life was as elsewhere.

Following George Leeds in 1900 were James Woodhouse 1900-1903, William Smith 1903-1905, Br Skyme 1905-1907, Albert Holmes 1907-1910, and Edgar Miskin 1910-1926.

Many a life was lost over the centuries and Phillip Benton in 1867 in the *History of the Rochford Hundred* wrote of 'a Mr Charles Miller, late surgeon of Great Wakering who, during his duties occasionally lost his way on the sands. However, he always used an old horse and when such an emergency arose, he threw the reins up and the horse's instincts never failed him'.

AWE (Foulness) Archaeological Society's study of the coastal habitat in a survey in 1974 revealed many buildings on Foulness of historic interest. The King's Head at Courtsend is said to be the oldest. Its origin was in the late 16th century; the alehouse licence was granted in 1589.

The Manorial Court sat in the Old Hall (Hall Farm) in Churchend. It was said that, after the Court's business was completed, the officials adjourned to the King's Head in Courtsend, no doubt overnight, to depart next morning for Fisherman's Head on to the Broomway.

Ridge Marsh Farm (Brick House) was built c1700, of brick with Flemish bond — probably the first brick building on the island. During the Napoleonic War there were two semaphore bases on the island, one at Burwood, the other near the King's Head. These bases were manned by the Rochford Hundred Volunteers, but such was the indiscipline, two signal cottages were erected to house the officers whose responsibility it was to maintain law and order among the unruly 'volunteers'.

The Volunteers were billeted just outside the Churchend village on the site of an old ale house known as Rochford Hundred Volunteers. There were at the time two other licensed premises, the George and Dragon and the King's Head. Mrs Amelia Bennewith held the licence of the RHV until 1815.

At the end of the Napoleonic War the building housing the Rochford Hundred Volunteers was sold and in 1825 became the Parish Poor House which, after the sale of the island in 1915, became known as the Workhouse Yard.

The Signal Cottage at Burwood was demolished but the Signal Cottage near the King's Head still stands and was extensively restored in 1995.

14

The Archaeological Society's research showed that Foulness appears to have developed in three stages; from mid to late 16th century; late 17th century and mid-19th century. Brick buildings appear to have been constructed as far back as the end of the 18th century and built of soft reds, which were probably transported by barge up the River Roach from the Stambridge Brickfields to the Quay loading. Buildings constructed of yellow stock bricks were probably built in the mid-19th century and the bricks transported across the sands from Shoeburyness.

The increase in population brought many problems, as many of the migrant labour force were fugitives from the law on the mainland. But the arrival of Rev Vachel in 1884 brought about a marked improvement and he was followed by Rev Samuel Dalton MA, who continued the good work. They were supported in their endeavours by Squire Finch, a well-respected man.

It was during this period that bare fist fights were commonplace, staged in the George and Dragon grounds, whose licensee was Amelia Bennewith, the mother of John Bennewith, the Foulness champion.

The Hall Farm House, venue for the Manorial Court
sittings in the 19th century.

Church magazine, 1898.

YESTERYEAR

An original source of information on Foulness is the 1898 *Fowlness* church monthly magazine — Foulness church choir prizes, donations to foreign missions, weddings and baptisms, a report on a pleasant evening enjoyed by the cricket club, all is there. Also featured were visits by mainland clergy, such as the rector of St Alban's Church, Prittlewell and an Easter Monday event when the Gardener family from a coastguard vessel anchored in the River Roach gave a concert in aid of church funds.

A visit to Windsor Castle on 9 June was said to have been 'most enjoyable, in view of the difficult journey', so one can assume it was a long day.

Cricket reports during the summer months figure prominently in the magazine and one fixture is of particular interest, when the visiting side came from Pentonville on a Whit Monday — the prison staff, presumably, not the inmates. It was an enjoyable day, for a member of the Pentonville team wrote 'I and the other lads say they never saw a more amiable lot of folk than the "Fowlness" people, I think they played first class cricket'.

Such information gives a valuable insight into the way of life on the Island in the 19th century, a small community, virtually cut off from the rest of the United Kingdom, yet endeavouring to keep in touch with the outside world.

Some years later a member of the Belton family travelled to the Lake District to purchase sheep. The transaction complete, he tried to send a telegram to the Foulness Post Office, but was informed that the Lake District Post Office had no record that such a place existed. One then realises the extent of the isolation prior to the construction of the bridge and road to the mainland in 1921/22.

The magazine goes on to report on a Sunday School treat for some 40 children who were to set sail for Burnham-on-Crouch; unfortunately, a Mr Fitch was unwell, so they had to ferry across the River Crouch and walk along the sea wall. Even that was not without incident for, while two crossings went well, the children had to be carried through the mud, which in places was two feet deep. They then had to travel to Southminster, where they were guests of the local vicar. Such ventures say a lot for the spirit and character of the Islanders.

To conclude that year's events, the children enjoyed a Sunday School treat on All Saints Day, with fireworks donated by Mr Dobson.

Foulness War Memorial.

WHERE TIME STANDS STILL

A column in a local paper, probably written shortly after the First
World War, gives a general view held by the 'Outsider' of life on the
Island. The article was headed:

'Island Where Time Stands Still
Foulness for a Real Rest Cure
Once a week Butcher

About 50 miles from London and about 10 miles or so from a well
known town lies a land where yesterday's paper are always today's
and where the post comes in and goes out at any hour.

This haven of rest is Foulness Island, off the marshy coast of Essex.

A roadway over the bed of the creek runs from Wakering Stairs,
near Shoeburyness, to the island. The natives call it The Broomway,
perhaps because of the branched tops of slender posts with which
the course is marked.

'The Postman's Thrill

Five miles in length and hidden beneath the sea at high water, the
Broomway is a perilous crossing, even for those who know it well.
The tide sweeps in with a rush and it's not long since a postman had
a narrow escape.

One middle-aged man, born and bred in the place, had never been
down to the spot where the bridge spans the creek.

The island possesses no doctor, no unemployment and the official
hour for the delivery of letters from Great Wakering varies with the
time of the daily tide.

For the despatch of the post, the times is five minutes prior to the
departure of the post for Wakering; this varies daily with the tide.

'Baker, but no Butcher

The island boasts a baker, no butcher. Every Friday a consignment
of meat comes up the river from Burnham on Crouch and Foulness
buys what it wants or goes without until the next batch arrives.

Most inhabitants are agricultural workers. They dwell in the isolated
farm houses or in isolated cottages set in the midst of an expanse of
open, treeless country.

The growing of clover and beans, table mustard and wheat, or
catching fish are the chief occupations of the folk who live there.

An auction of household furniture is a thing unheard of, a removal
is a rarity and strangers are regarded with marked interest.

Foulness is a land of solitude and peace, of far off sea birds' cries,
and salt air stings the cheeks.

IT IS A PLACE WHERE TIME STANDS STILL'

Columnist C.H.E.B. wrote about the island as he saw it, but with little knowledge of the Foulness people for, as this story unfolds, readers will realise that the writer, like so many others, had been poorly briefed.

Foulness Island, like so many village communities, certainly held those who never wished to leave their home area. At the same time, although it may have been isolated, its people never lacked a spirit of adventure and over the years, many left to seek their fortunes elsewhere.

Several come to mind, such as 'Sagy' Rawlings, who became a sergeant in the Metropolitan Police; James Dobson, who joined the Police in Pimlico and a member of the Cripps family, who served in the London Fire Service.

More important, the island played its part in World War I. Its men served on the Somme and the European front and as far afield as Mesopotamia and seven gave their lives for the country, with more sad losses in the Second World War. The war memorial at the entrance to the churchyard of St Mary's pays a fitting tribute to the men who died.

Still well maintained in the '90s in a sadly neglected churchyard, it bears the following inscriptions and the names of the Islander who gave their lives for their country:

'To the Glory of God
and in the grateful remembrance of the men from the
parish who fell in the First World War 1914-18
Bert Boosey
William Hammett
George Dyer
Fred Rawlings
Fred Bush
Henry Threadgold'
'To the Glory of God
and in the grateful remembrance of the men from this
parish who fell in the Second World War 1939-45.
Lewis Belton
Raymond Cook
Frank Hume'

To lose such a number of its young men must have been a sad and traumatic experience for such a small and isolated community.

The sea and fear of floods were realities of life. On one occasion in the '20s, the Sunday morning service was interrupted with a call from the pulpit for the menfolk to leave and go to the sea wall to help repair a break in the sea defences. Such events, coupled with the remoteness of the island, never deterred inhabitants from endeavouring to make the best of their lives, on the land or afloat on barges. A typical example of resourcefulness was shown by my late father, who started work at the age of eleven and was a self-taught wheelwright who, when the need arose, travelled across the Broomway to the East End of London to purchase wheel naves for the construction of local farm carts.

It was quite common for the young ladies of the island to travel across the sands *via* the Broomway, single-handedly driving a pony and trap. This was a hazardous journey for the most hardened individual, but Foulness inhabitants were an indomitable breed.

Postman leaving the Stairs, Great Wakering, to cross the sand *via* the Broomway.

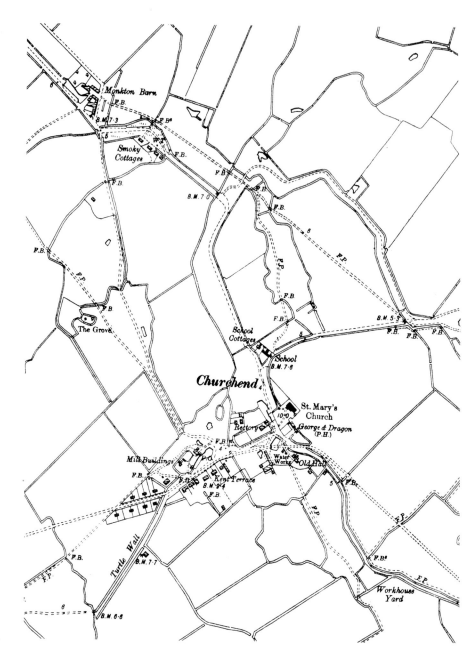

Churchend, from the 1920 OS map.

AN ISLAND TOUR

Visiting the island, one had the choice of two forms of entry: across the sands at low tide from Great Wakering, which was no route for the faint-hearted, or by sea to the Quay Loading from the River Roach. Once arrived, there was a climb up slippery steps, when at low tide the seaweed made the ascent precarious, even for the most able.

Glancing over the sea wall, one soon realises that Foulness is distinctly different, a vast area of flat land, almost devoid of trees and with few hedgerows, an area of around 7,000 acres with a coastline of 14 miles of high sea walls. Yet it has a charm of its own.

Visitors would have seen below the wall an expanse of water known as 'the fleet', which continued around the island as a second line of defence against the sea coming over the wall during gale-force winds, the water returning to the rivers at low tide through the numerous sluice gates around the island.

Summer visitors could well have become enchanted with their very different view of the peaceful landscape — hardly a sound to be heard except for the abundance of island birds. The fields could be a mass of colour, sheaves stacked and awaiting the wagons, or lucerne in full bloom and perhaps an expanse of golden mustard.

Winter visitors might well have encountered an entirely different environment. Winds from the North Sea could be bitter and, with many of the paths little more than grass tracks, the newly-arrived would be anxious to get to the villages without delay.

Leaving the Quay, the route would continue to the Quay Farm, where 'Wick' Shelley and his family resided, on through the farm yard and by plank bridge over a stream to Smokey Cottages.

There were eight cottages, at various times occupied by the families of the Cripps, Pottons, Manning, Self, Whisken — and Snelgrove, the Customs Officer. Tourists could not help but notice a ramshackle building, which housed Tubby Manning's pony. All were demolished after the Second World War.

Leaving Smokey, their route crossed over to the grass track on to the Brick Hills, possibly the site of a brickfield many years ago and hardly hills, more of a mound. After the 'Hills', one passed the 15-acre Glebe field, then the school field, the scene of so much childhood enjoyment. Through the kissing gate and to the right stood the school cottages and St Mary's Church of England School. These cottages were demolished soon after World War II.

Due north of the school playing field lay the Pound, used to shelter the cattle. Between this and Naze Wick Farm was a levelled area, which up to the early '20s was the local cricket ground. It was ideally situated; one could imagine the home side on a Saturday afternoon anxiously scanning the horizon for the first sight of the visitors travelling from the Quay Loading.

On leaving the school, the stroller would come to the first of many well-maintained paths, a surface of cockle shells, found in abundance on the shell banks of the eastern coast. To the left of the path on the way to the western entrance of the Churchyard was a deep ditch and the extension to the cemetery. At the gate, one would have seen a wooden structure which, contrary to the view of visiting scribes, was not a lock-up, but a mortuary to shelter the bodies of shipwrecked seamen. Alas, this was all too frequent during that period and at times an unpleasant task for the locals, who were paid a sum of money to 'moor' the deceased. This building was replaced during the rebuilding programme of the '20s.

Eventually a path was diverted across the corner, much to the relief of the children, who always gave that particular building a wide berth.

Directly opposite was the Rectory and a large pond, which was often frozen over and the scene of winter sports for school children. From there one would leave the Church's southern gate and the recently erected war memorial and see the George and Dragon Inn, usually the first port of call for seafarers and yachtsmen from Burnham.

Pausing for a while under the huge elm tree, a regular meeting place for local youth, one would join the tree-lined path on the edge of the vicarage ground. Then one came to the entrance to the garden of a weather-boarded bungalow, which housed the Government agent, the last being Jack Taylor. The bungalow, said to be of Dutch origin, was demolished in the rebuilding programme and a pair of a more modern design erected.

Opposite were the Round Gardens, playground for local children. In the immediate post-war period, before new homes were built, the path crossed what was known as the Stinking Ditch and came to the village shop, the Mill. Continuing through the Mill garden, one came to a rundown cottage, then occupied by Jimmy Dowsett, who was said to be the island's oldest cyclist. This cottage was eventually demolished, then rebuilt and occupied by Ernest Wallace, son of the owner of the shop.

The Windmill is said in photographs to have been 400 years old, but the County Records say otherwise. By 1915 it was dilapidated and was demolished, as it was thought it might be a landmark for the enemy, overlooking the fact that the tower of St Mary's Church rose many feet higher.

Before and immediately after the First World War, the village of Churchend comprised a cluster of boarded cottages and a pair of brick-built houses, occupied at the time by the Humes and the Webbs. Next door was the old shop, a weather-boarded building from which Isiah Belton traded. This was in time knocked down and a more modern pair of dwellings erected.

Along the wooden terraced row, still occupied in the '90s, were families of Webbs, Rippingale, Farr and Cripps, the Webb family having resided there for over 150 years. The last of the line, Miss Phoebe Webb, died in September 1994.

The first post-war rebuilding took place due north of the terraced row, with homes for the district nurse and the village policeman among others and an enlarged house and an extension known by historians as a bothy, although locally the extensions were known as the 'mens' kitchen'. This extension was intended to house farmhands, but was never used. When the Mill shop was demolished after the Second World War it became the Post Office.

Next to the police house, the War Department installed its maintenance yard and the employees became known as 'on check'. The yard survived until the Second World War.

The new brick buildings were something of a design experiment, built with stock bricks and with cavity wall insulation. They also had flush toilets, the first on the island, as well as indoor taps and a bath. Although the toilets were connected to a purifying plant, the outflow was into a neighbouring ditch, which left much to be desired, hence the name of 'the stinking ditch'.

In this redevelopment period, a new blacksmith's forge was built opposite the boarded terraced row, also in stock bricks and this replaced the old blacksmith's at Bethlehem Row. Mr Dowsett and his son, Alf, had the business until it closed some years later. Still further buildings were erected to the south of the village in the mid '20s, built with a brick inner skin and boarded externally, but with no flush toilets.

Leaving Churchend, one would travel along what was known in that period as Turtle Road, nothing more than a cart track with a grass footpath. It would have passed Rugwood and Priestwood Farms, the latter run by Mr Belcham and during the early '20s occupied by Mr George Bird. The Dowsett family lived in Rugwood Farm.

During the redevelopment period, the Ministry of Defence erected a modern brick-built stable alongside the Turtle Road, intended for the Royal Artillery horses, but never used.

From Rugwood a farm track led to Rugwood Head, yet another exit to the Broomway, passing through Bethlehem Row, demolished during the early post-war years. The footpath from Rugwood Farm went south to Burrow Woods Farm and there resided a member of the Manning family and another occupant. Originally old cottages, they were replaced with a similar design to the southern end of Churchend.

Then on to New House Farm, occupied by Fred Lilley and family and from there to the headways of Shelford and Asplins; leaving the farm, a grass path took one due west to the Jerry Wood, which stood then much as it does in the '90s, showing no sign of occupation in previous years. Then to Great Shelford; that was occupied by the Willsmer family, and Little Shelford, a pair of remote brick houses, occupied at times by the Bartrams, the Smiths and the Turners, all working on the neighbouring farm.

The next stop was at Smallgains Farm at the south western corner of the island. This was occupied at the time by the Cottis, Pavitt and Chapman families. There was the main house, a pair of brick-built houses designed like those in Churchend, and adjacent to them a weather-boarded house. The farm buildings at Great Shelford and Little Shelford, as well as Smallgains, were demolished in the late '40s to make way for a research establishment.

Smallgains Farm was the tenancy of Douglas Smith, an offshore tenant, whose family had an interesting structure sitting on the sea wall north of Smallgains — a complete rail carriage used for summer holidays. It rested there until the late '40s, when it was removed and reappeared on the sea wall off the Burnham marches. Its removal and erection was no mean feat in those days.

Leaving Smallgains, one travelled along the sea wall to the ruins of White House Farm and past White House Hole, which was virtually an extension to the sea wall, creating an enclosed area, no doubt constructed at the time when the wall was breached by the sea. From there one came to the Quay Loading and to the Quay Farm and then on to the original route.

Alternatively, one could leave Smallgains and return to Churchend, *via* New Marsh Farm along the usual grass path. The Farm was then occupied by the Whisken family. *En route* one would have passed Old Barns or Small Ports, a veritable bird sanctuary, home to coots and herons living in peace in the reeds.

Travellers to Courtsend from the rivers could visit the Quays near the village, but landing at the Quay Loading off Quay Farm, one would make one's way *via* Smokey Cottages to the Naze Wick Farm, which consisted of two houses occupied by the farmer, Mr Charles Cater and Mr Jim Dow and a mens' section. Next to the farmhouse was a metal-constructed windmill, erected to pump water, which was a source not only for the farm, but in the past for residents of the Workhouse Yard.

Leaving the farm and travelling north to the river Crouch, one came across the Crouch Cottages erected under the lee-side of the sea wall and the homes of the Rawlings and Riley families. These places were sheltered from northerly winds, but the protection was insufficient to prevent loss of life in the floods of 1953, when Mrs Rawlings, a war widow, was drowned.

From Crouch Corner, a rough farm track leads to Brick House Farm and on to Buttons Row, a row of semi-detached dwellings still in occupation in the '90s, then Shelley's Row, where Mr Bird had a small general store.

Among the residents was Mick O'Keefe and close by was Blacksmith's Row and the farrier's business run by Mr Threadgold and his son, Frank. The business ceased trading with the coming of the tractor and the row was demolished in the '30s.

Way off in the distance, due north east and near Foulness Point, was East Newlands, the home of the Nichols family. From there children probably had the longest trek to the village school of any of the island's youngsters.

Leaving the Blacksmith's Row, the visitor, soon after the First World War, would come to a development of houses built to the Kent design, with two skins of concrete panels. They were occupied by the Meads, Shelleys, Birds and others. Next on this route came the King's Head Inn. The licensee then was Mr Whent, who also farmed the nearby twenty or so acres. Close by was the Signal Cottage, at long last restored in 1994. It was part of the defence strategy in the period of the Napoleonic wars. The occupants at the end of the First World War were Mr Webb and his daughter, Daisy.

Leaving the King's Head one came across a building almost covered in ivy. The shop was owned by Miss Louise Ballenger, a relation of the Guivers, who had the George and Dragon in Churchend. When she retired, the shop was demolished and replaced by a purpose-built one near the original site, and the tenancy was taken over by Walter Hawkes, who also took over the twenty acres attached to the Inn. The shop flourished for some years but, after the Second World War, reverted to a house. A few yards further south was a cluster of cottages occupied by well-known local families, including the Rippingales. Nearby stood a single-storey building, the Chapel, known as St Luke's and living next door was the family of 'Tidder' Nichols.

On the rise near the houses stood the home of the local harness maker, Mr Mead, affectionately known as 'Hawley'. He was also part-time rate collector for the Rochford Rural District Council and a church warden. Mr Mead was a typical example of the fine rural craftsmen of the day, famed for his green lunch bags, widely sought after by the working population.

Due east, one passed the 'Skirts', the village football field, then on to Fisherman's Head, passing West Newlands. Fisherman's Head was the main exit to the Broomway and, as the name suggests, used by the local fishermen. It was also used frequently by the Royal Artillery based at the Shoeburyness firing ranges, when horses were used to pull the gun carriages across the sands at low tide. Also sited near the Head were stables, small barracks and a bungalow. It was here, when you glanced across the sands on a sunny summer's day, that you realised the tour was all worthwhile, for here was a view for many miles, with freighters in the distance, far off from the shore, and an expanse of sand which, at low tide, allowed one to enjoy the peace and quiet of the Maplin, broken only by the cries of sea birds. A few hours here was a sure cure for insomnia.

Tracing the route back, one came to Tree Farm, known by historians as New House Farm, said to be the oldest of the island's houses. The writer's ancestor resided there at the time of the 1851 census, registered as the farm bailiff. In the post-war period the families of the Birds and Willsmers lived there.

Leaving Tree Farm, travelling due south along the usual farm track, the next stop was East Wick Farm and the residents were the families of 'Buddy' Banks and George Cottis. Nearby stood a row of boarded cottags with the usual tar decor and among the residents was the Webb family. A few yards west was an attractive old cottage with a white snowcem exterior and there lived Basil Dobson, a horseman on the farm. The farmhouse had the usual mens' quarters and a well known character known as Joby resided there.

A few hundred yards south of East Wick on the old sea wall stood Foxes, originally listed as a farm and sold as such in the 1915 sale of the island. In that period it was incorporated with the main farm and the last resident was said to have been Stan Shelley. All these properties were demolished in the late '30s.

Wishing to return directly to Churchend, one could have travelled along the winding paths adjacent to the numerous fields, all known to the locals by their acreage. The writer can still recall, never to be forgotten, the location of the Five Acre and the Twenty Eight. However, the tour would be more interesting if one traced one's steps back *via* Tree Farm to the centre of Courtsend and returned *via* the winding path to New Wick Farm, home of the Hume and Kirby famlies. The farm was a Guiver tenancy.

On to the Lodge Farm, farmed by Walter Cater and, by island standards a stately home, which also had the usual annex for the farm hands; it is still there, well maintained.

Along the well-trodden path returning to Churchend, one comes to the Workhouse Yard, a terraced row of boarded cottages in the usual decor and all facing a common yard. Little is known of their origin. Perhaps the name is self-explanatory, but it was a subject not spoken of among the family. The clue to their use is borne out by the fact that the writer's grandfather was a resident of the Quay Farm in the late 1890s, a tied house. When he died, grandmother, with a large family, was forced to leave and the family moved to the Workhouse Yard. There information dries up, although my father once said he slept there on a straw bed. After 1915 there were no longer any tied cottages on the Island; all houses were rented from the War Department.

At the entrance to the Workhouse Yard was a small cottage, which was the home of the district nurse. At that time it was Nurse Bowman. Other residents in the Yard in the early post-war years were the families of the Humes, Shelleys and, for a short period, the Perrins, who came from the East End of London during the recession.

Finally, one arrived at Hall Farm, where lived Isiah Belton. Even in those times it was an impressive building, facing south and overlooking the farm. Adjacent were the men's quarters, not in use at the time and shortly to be converted to a dwelling place for Mr Bert Belton. Near the farmhouse was the pumping station for the local water supply, still standing, but not in use since the mains water supply came to the island soon after the Second World War. This was in many ways regrettable, as the water was pleasant to drink and extremely soft.

As for the plant, it was the pride and joy of the engineer, Teddy Nichols, who was followed by Perrin, then for a brief period by Frank Wakefield, who left to open the well-known garage in Shoeburyness of Wakefield and Sage. The last engineer was Perce Ventris.

Finally, looking over our shoulders, we see the George and Dragon Inn, in those days looking externally much as it does today in the '90s, but of course, much has changed apart from the prices. At that time the landlords were Bert and Harry Guiver, who were said to be of independent means, apart from farming several farms on the Island. It was a hobby in many ways, but it proved a most welcome rest for visiting yachtsmen and bargemen from the Rivers Crouch and Roach.

Looking at the map of the Island and the route taken, one can see the results of progress or change arising from military needs. Gone are the most outlying houses. Those who remember the way it was cannot help but feel a trifle sad.

ABOVE: The George & Dragon Inn. BELOW: White House Farm and the Dowsett family.

ABOVE: Early post-World War I house in Churchend.
BELOW: Southern Churchend.

ABOVE: Bethlehem Row. BELOW: New House Farm,
with members of the Bush family.

ABOVE: George Cottis's wedding and BELOW: that of
the Pavitts.

ABOVE: Mr Threadgold snr on wheel repairs. BELOW:
Blacksmith's Row, Courtsend.

ABOVE: Shoeing horses at Mr Threadgold's. BELOW:
The King's Head Inn, Courtsend.

ABOVE: Courtsend village near the chapel, and
BELOW: near the harness makers.

ABOVE: Sara Cole at Lt Newlands. BELOW: Shepherd's
Hut near New Wick Farm.

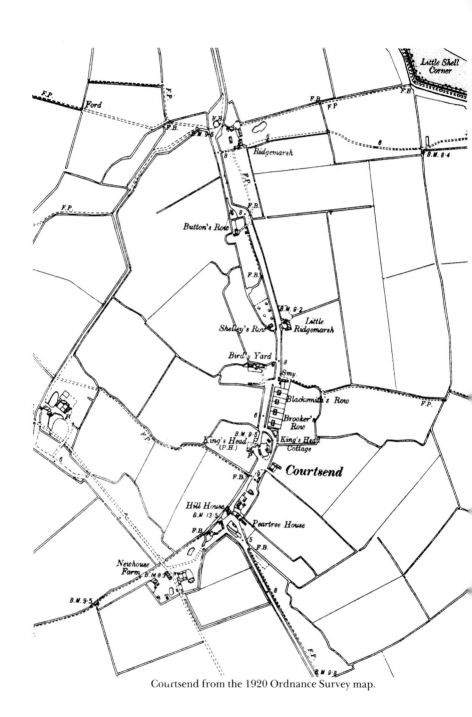

Courtsend from the 1920 Ordnance Survey map.

THE BURNHAM CONNECTION

Burnham-on-Crouch over the centuries was virtually the only connection the Island had with the mainland, apart from the Broomway across the sands. Indeed the forefathers of many an islander, including my own, had come over from the Dengie Hundred area. Many had relatives in Burnham, so there was always a close relationship between the two communities.

It was more than that; it was a partnership of sheer necessity, for Foulness relied heavily on Burnham for its worldly goods. The late George Clark, former Editor of the local paper, gave me, some years ago, a graphic illustration of the Burnham connection, describing how in the holiday periods as a youngster he was allowed to accompany Ike Harvey on his regular run to Foulness.

The day commenced by collecting the groceries from Luckin Smith's and the meat from Osborn's, which was loaded from the town steps on to a gaff-rigged pleasure boat, either the *Favourite* or the *Water Lilley*, then down they sailed to the Branklet and turned up the River Roach.

A mile on they landed at the Quay Loading which, according to the tide, could be extremely dangerous. Once ashore, they began the long trek to Churchend or, as George Clark mentioned, a call to the George and Dragon. He described the route as nothing more than a farm track and across numerous plank bridges, so such a journey made the visit to the George and Dragon a priority.

Mr Clark also recalled how periodically a Mr Westhorp accompanied them. He was in the drapery trade, taking orders and delivering the following week. Other members of the Harvey family were also frequent visitors to the Island. Apart from the Quay, loading points were also used near Courtsend, most common being the Crouch and Clark's Hard.

Summertime saw the use of the Burnham motor boats by the local cricket club, visiting opponents in Burnham, Paglesham, Southminster and Bradwell. George Bourne also hired his boat, the strangely named *Ucmeopit*, taking visitors to the annual show on Foulness. Such visits continued until 1939. Burnham children also went to the Island as an annual Sunday School treat.

Although Foulness ceased to be so dependent on Burnham after 1922, with the opening of the bridge and the road, the relationship was certainly not forgotten. During the terrible East Coast floods of 1953, Burnham folk came to the islanders' rescue.

A Burnham resident informed me that during that awful time, he and others were checking on the plight of Wallasea residents. Mission completed, they enquired the fate of Foulness people and were told that the military were looking after them but, to their surprise, on the radio that very evening, they learnt there were still people on Foulness waiting to be rescued.

News flashed around Burnham and a local GP, a Dr Wilson, called for volunteers to muster at the Burnham Quay at seven the next morning. By dawn the response was overwhelming and at eight o'clock they were off the Quay Loading at Foulness, pulling the dinghies over the wall. They rescued stranded people and took them to the Royal Corinthian Yacht Club. They were cared for by the ladies of the Burnham branch of the Womens's Voluntary Servcie, while the town's menfolk continued with Operation Animal Rescue, their crafts being more suitable for the task than the military ones.

It is a pleasant thought that after all those years, the relationship remains as strong as in the past.

Burnham Quay.

ABOVE: Floods in Churchend, 1953. BELOW: 1953
floods taken from No 16 Churchend showing the Old
Shop across the pond.

41

'Leaving for England' from Fisherman's Head.

TAYLOR'S DREAM

The beginning of the First World War in 1914 was really the end of almost complete isolation for Foulness Island and a new dawn. Since 1890, when the Old Ranges were installed at Shoeburyness, the use of the sands as a firing range had become something of a problem to both the military and the islanders, for the question of safety often arose for those using the Broomway. The route *via* Wakering Stairs to and from Foulness Island was already hazardous enough, without the fear of shell fragments falling around travellers.

Serious thoughts were given to the clash of interests and several projects were considered. Military historian Tony Hill, a retired Royal Artillery Major, wrote in *The Shoe* in 1982 that building a road had been considered. That was in 1911 but, until the outbreak of war in 1914, little had been done. Then the War Department decided to buy Foulness and the New England Islands and the contracts were completed in 1915.

Major Hill also supplies some interesting data about the conveyancing, reporting that Squire Finch, as the major landowner, sold some 4,000 acres for £70,000; Southend Luker's Brewery sold the George and Dragon inn in Churchend for £500; Rev Hole sold the Glebe, a 15-acre field near the school cottages, for £320. Another landmark, the Old Windmill in Churchend, owned by Mrs Judd and Miss Curtiss, went for £500. Other transactions included the sale of Brickhouse Farm and New Marsh Farm for £6,500, as well as Bethlehem Row and Old Barns for £950.

Also recorded were the sale of Foxes Farm and land owned by Mrs M. A. Guiver (Marcote coal) for £1,150 and White House Farm sold by J. Hepburn for £16,250. Later Hepburn was to lose his tenancies due to his alleged German connections. It was said he had employed a German to advise on growing sugar beet on his farm. The fact is that little tolerance was shown in the early days of the war. Arising from this decision, Great and Little Newlands, Tree Farm and Ridgemarsh Farm were taken over by the Beltons and the Guivers.

So, at long last the die was cast and Foulness was to lose its isolation. In August 1915 a contract was placed with Findlay & Co Ltd, roof and bridge builders of Motherwell, Scotland for the supply and erection of a Scherzer Rolling Lift Bridge, the designers being an American company from Chicago.

Copies of the contract destroy the long-held myth believed by many regarding the origin of the bridge. It was thought to have been a German bridge, part of the post-war reparations. At least it made interesting conversation at the time.

This was an epic era in the history of Foulness, a construction project designed and supervised by the Royal Engineers, using direct labour. This undertaking was worthy of comparison to the construction of the Manchester Ship Canal, for the conditions were extremely unusual and difficult, as well as being harsh for both the employees and their supervisors. They had to endure the bitter winds coming from the North Sea in an area where it was once said it was the only place on earth where the rain was horizontal; yet construction continued throughout the winters of 1920/22.

Little mechanisation was available so much of the work was done with pick and shovel. To assist in transportation, a light railway brought the building material from Shoeburyness and bogies fitted with diesel engines were also used. To supplement the supply side, barges brought in supplies to the Quay Loading area and were then transported on a narrow gauge track to Churchend.

The labour force included a considerable contingent from Burnham on Crouch, who were billeted in Army huts at Priestwood Farm in the days of George Bird, who at the time was the farm resident. The Burnham men were brought by boat every Monday morning. Among the recruits were several well-known Burnham names: Tunbridge, Harvey, Trussell, Chittick (died in 1994) and King. Among them were some of the members of the popular local football team, Burnham Ramblers and on each Saturday those members hastened home to don the local colours.

Dams were built to keep out the North Sea, the main one being that which crosses Shelford Creek and is next to the present highway. To facilitate this vast engineering project, it was essential to have efficient supply lines so, before reclamation of New England Island, a trestle bridge was built by driving piles into the mud and fixing cross-members, on which a rail track was laid to continue to the Jerry Wood, some two miles north. The piles were visible above the mud long after the bridge ceased to be used; the track was used by what was known as 'The Scooter'.

This temporary structure close to the main road was mentioned in the *Royal Engineers' Journal*, December 1925. It said 'its length was some 650 yards and was the innocent cause of the purchase of some 200-300 bicycles by the islanders, many of whom had never visited the mainland'.

Pile driving was taking place in 1916, but the completion date was not recorded and the Royal Engineers faced unforseen problems, so it was unlikely the bridge was officially opened before 1921/22.

During the construction of the Findlay Bridge, the caretaker's house was erected near the northern end of the bridge crossing Havengore Creek. It was a unique house, the first built to the design patented by the retired Col Kent of the Royal Engineers. This was based on the pier and panel principle; the piers were reinforced concrete and the panels were long slim slabs, the two skins forming a 5″ cavity. The same design was used in the redevelopment of Courtsend, where the row was sometimes known as Kent's Row.

Jim Cork was the first bridgekeeper, a man of considerable strength; he had to be, as the bridge was manually lifted with a hand-winding mechanism to allow the free passage of vessels out to sea. It was some years before the winding gear was electrically operated.

Life on the bridge had its moments and Jim had to be available at all hours according to the time of the tide, ever ready to raise the bridge for sailing boats. It had its compensations, but not always according to plan. One incident relates to an occasion when one of the island residents, Mr Reg Rawlings, was returning from the mainland and found the bridge up so, while passing the time away, he casually kicked a matchbox into the creek, thinking it was litter. Soon the bridge was down and Jim appeared from the winding platform. Looking around he shouted at Reg, 'where's my matchbox?' Alas, the matchbox contained a gratuity from a grateful yachtsman!

As for the road, the late Jack Taylor wrote an interesting article for the house journal of the BRC Company. He was the resident Clerk of Works on Foulness, a talented constructional engineer. His *The Road Makers of Foulness* explains how the BRC solved the age-old riddle of the sands. Reading the article, one gets a feeling for the enthusiasm of the writer. His description of the island vividly captures its romantic isolation and he mentions its eerie mystery, akin to Dickens' description of the black marshes in his *Great Expectations*.

Another graphic description of a journey across the Broomway, the danger and the loss of life, confirms why he became convinced of the need for the coming of the road. That statutory declaration, made by Mr Fred Lilley in 1915, related to the death of Emmanuel Holmes, and emphasised the danger of travelling to Foulness *via* the Broomway. Mr Holmes, although within shouting distance of the sea wall, nonetheless became confused and lost his life.

Mr Holmes' son, Bob, resided in Churchend and attended the Foulness school in the 1920s. Mr Rogers lived at Rugwood and, after his tragic death in 1915, the family moved off the island.

Jack Taylor writes of the immense construction problems and that the answer would be the use of BRC metal fabric in 6″-7″

concrete. His enthusiasm for this method of constructional engineering was boundless, despite the problems faced by the road-makers in what was virtually a battle against the elements.

At last New England was reclaimed from the sea and had its concrete road which, Taylor boasted, would be the finest in Essex. Local critics had been mistrustful of the whole venture, for they were only too well aware of the nature of the soil and the local environment. But it went ahead and was completed in 1922.

According to Jack Taylor, Sunday papers were delivered the same day as they were published. 'Taylor's Dream' had come true. He might well have said 'Mission Completed'.

There was a sequel to the road construction, when concrete use of this kind was in its infancy, for in the '30s, during a hot summer, the road lifted, as the writer can verify. While travelling home at the end of day from Southend, he was confronted by a section of the road near Priestwood Farm having risen about three feet, enabling one to crawl underneath.

It was alleged by some at the time that the fault lay in an unstable foundation, but it was more likely to have been caused by insufficient expansion strips, for concrete can expand half an inch for every 100 feet. The problem was rectified and the road gave little trouble in the years to come; Taylor's dream had become reality. Life on the island changed beyond all recognition. Public transport soon arrived, provided by Westcliff Motors with a service one on and off each Friday and five on Saturday. Such was the new-found freedom. The 'buses were extremely popular with those wishing to do the weekly shopping, a visit to the numerous cinemas in Southend, or perhaps the Kursaal football ground, the home of Southend United. The fares to Southend were 1s 7d return from Churchend and 1s 9d return from Courtsend.

Eventually public transport was followed by private and the Great Wakering doctor came over on a motor cycle, a far cry from the days when he used to cross the sands to visit his patients. The District Nurse, Nurse Bowman, acquired what was known as a Ner-a-car, a motorised scooter; others soon became proud owners of motor cycles. A constant stream of locals made their way to and from the mainland.

With the arrival of transport, came a new industry, the 'cycle repair shop. 'Judy' Finch set up business in Churchend which, apart from a repair shop, included a modest window display of spare parts and accessories and a Raleigh cycle. This and the Hercules, a much cheaper 'cycle, were the most common.

'Judy' was an indomitable character, quite unflappable. In his case time stood still if he so wished. He was mainly self-taught, as was the case of most islanders, able to turn his hand to any task that might arise. The remoteness of the island probably had a lot to do with it. Quietly confident in all he did and conscientious to extremes, the customer could always count on a first class job, provided of course that the customer did not mind waiting.

As with all Foulness men, 'Judy' was of an independent nature. As time passed he purchased an Austin car. For years it was his pride and joy and he branched out into the taxi business. He was always reliable and his charges were moderate. He was renowned for never rushing a journey; it was doubtful if he ever exceeded 30 miles per hour.

During the ensuing years, his workshop was often a haven for locals during the long winter evenings. A call lasted hours, a nut tightened here, a screw turned with a casual grunt, always with a fag drooping ever lower, watched by an audience who had little else to do, every move carefully studied, the silence broken only by reference to latest local gossip. Alas, like so many others before him, 'Judy' came to a sad end. He had been attending to his fishing lines some distance out on the Maplin sands when he was found dead.

In the mid-1920s radio arrived on the island — nothing as sophisticated as we know today, but the humble crystal set, used with headphones, a simple affair, measuring about eight cubic inches in size and comprising a crystal and the 'cat's whisker'. With careful manipulation of the whisker to the correct position on the crystal one could receive the London Radio Station 2LO, with Henry Hall's band heard for the first time in many island homes, but woe betide any movement near the set, for the station could be lost. Soon, like the mainland, the island radio listeners moved on.

It was as though one had entered a new world, the ultimate end of the island's complete isolation and the people took it all in their stride when the one valve sets arrived, followed by the two and three valve sets with the Blue Spot speakers. Houses were then adorned with outside aerials, comprising two strands of wire between two poles, the higher, the better. It was to become the status symbol of the age. But these sets required power and mains electricity had yet to arrived on the island. In fact, Foulness did not go on to the National Grid until after the Second World War.

To overcome this problem, a battery was needed, together with an accumulator, which needed recharging regularly. This is where the ever-dependable 'Judy' came in, for he supplied this service by taking the accumulators to 'Ticket's' in Great Wakering for recharging.

By this time bicycles were a must and our local entrepreneur did a roaring trade, both with the old and the young. The oldest cyclist at the time was Jimmy Dowsett, then in his '80s, which goes to show that none of the residents were prepared to be left behind. Even on Foulness, 'cycle lamps were required. These were a necessity, because deep ditches ran alongside the winding paths. The lamps range from the Silver King oil lamp, now a collector's item , to the more enterprising gas lamp. This type had a container which held carbide crystals and the upper section was filled with water, which was controlled and released on to the crystals, creating a gas. When ignited, this provided a good light.

The Scherzer Rolling Bridge over Havengore Creek.

48

ABOVE: The bridge over New England at high tide on
the Scooter. BELOW: Building the road over New
England.

ABOVE: The temporary trestle bridge near D. Dam.
BELOW: Workmen on the road near the Vicarage,
Churchend.

50

I, FREDERICK WALTER LILLEY of Foulness in the County of Essex, Farm Bailiff do hereby solemnly and sincerely declare as follows:-

1. I have lived on Foulness Island all my life and am well acquainted with the broomway across the sands leading from the Island to Great Wakering which can only be used when the tide is out.

2. I knew Emanuel Holmes of Great Wakering who is believed to have lost his life when attempting to cross to Foulness on the afternoon of the Sixth November 1915. Late in the afternoon of that day I was at my home near to New House Headway on the Island when I heard cries for help in a man's voice from the direction of the sands near the broomway. It was foggy and also getting dark at the time and the man who must have been some considerable distance away could not be seen but I shouted to him as loud as I could to let him

to cross over the sands and a number of lives have been lost in making the attempt. On the fifteenth of March of this year a Foulness man named William Rogers who knew the sands and broomway well lost his life when attempting to drive from Wakering to the Island late at night and his body was not found for some days later AND I make this solemn declaration

conscientiously believing the same to be true and by virtue of the

DECLARED by the above named Frederick) Statutory Declarations Act
Walter Lilley at *Southend on Sea*) 1835.
in the County of *Essex*.)
this *5th* day of *April* 1917) *H. W. Lilley*
)

Before me,

M. T. Drysdale

Statutory Declaration by Frederick Walter Lilley on the
'missing presumed drowned' tragedy of Emanuel Holmes
— 5 April 1917.

51

ABOVE: Churchend in the 1920s. BELOW: 'Judy' Fitch's
workshop and car.

HORSE AND HARVEST

During the Great War and the 1920s, life on the farm went along at a leisurely pace, with sowing in the winter and spring and reaping in the summer. Ploughing in those days was by a single plough, pulled by a pair of Shire horses. It was an impressive sight when the horsemen, the élite of the farm employees, lined up at the head of the field, with horses well-groomed, bedecked with ribbons and polished brass work.

Soon after the war, the Shire horses were replaced by the lighter Suffolks, a handsome breed, some actually raised by the Belton family. However, as always, change had its critics, who thought the Suffolks would be unable to cope with the heavy island soil. Their fears proved groundless and the Suffolks reigned supreme until the tractor arrived in the 1930s and the 'Boxers' and 'Turpins' of the stables became redundant.

The task of ploughing was supplemented to some extent by the use of steam traction engines. The Guiver brothers had a pair operatred by Mr Bird and Mr Dyer. The Smoothy family of Rochford also hired out engines to Foulness farmers.

The practice was a simple one. An engine was posted on each side of the field and a steel cable was attached to the drum on each. This hauled the plough, with its several shears, to and fro across the fields. After each crossing the engines moved forward. It worked well when conditions made the normal horse plough unsuitable; but, being coal-fired, it was labour intensive.

The island was farmed by seven farmers and was a patchwork of fields and areas. Routes and distances always related to the acreage, a practice recognised by all the locals. This was a period when white crops followed black: wheat, oats and barley, after mustard and beans. The fields were systematically set aside for a season of fallow, to allow the soil to recover. This was good husbandry, but in the following years the practice was mostly abandoned in the cause of greater productivity, without regard to the long term future.

Those fields of mustard, corn and lucerne surely would have made an impressive aerial photograph, for theirs was a veritable patchwork quilt effect. There were sixteen farms in the early 1920s and they were the main source of employment. The hours were long and hard, especially from the spring until the end of harvest, but that was the general practice of employees, who stayed with a farmer for most of their working lives. The writer can recall the sound of the footsteps of horsemen passing at the crack of dawn, going into the farmyard to feed their horses before the hard day ahead.

There was always a close bond between the horseman and his charges and one can be sure there was an element of sadness when the tractors took over, compensated, no doubt, by the fact that the work was a bit lighter.

A local horseman at the Hall Farm, when he referred to the usual practice at the weekend, once remarked 'you just watch them when they finish work on Saturday' and, true to form, the horses galloped out of the farmyard, pausing at the mill pond for a drink and then on, through the gate, to the Grove field. The gate was shut behind them. This was their weekend ritual.

On Sunday the horses could be seen gazing over the gate towards the village, but on Monday, just as the horsemen forecast, not a horse was in sight. They were at the other end of the Grove field, a mile or so in the distance. One might well say 'They knows, yer know'.

Reading Jack Taylor's article, *The Roadmakers of Foulness*, one realises the importance of horses in the daily life of Foulness in the years before the road to the mainland was built. He writes of the romantic isolation, of the black marshes and the nature of the soil — a loamy substance, different from the mainland. In that period there were no pavements or hard roads, just primitive tracks. Pictures of the period show that it took no fewer than thirteen powerful Shire horses to move a hay press from one field to another.

Most of the fields were surrounded by ditches, many deep and tidal, often crossed by a single plank. They were well-maintained, which was essential due to the nature of the soil. Ploughing was done to a pattern different to that on the mainland. The fields were ploughed in stetches and drained across with furrows into the ditch; rarely was a field under water.

The climax of the farming year was the annual harvest, a period when all sporting activities ceased and the priority was to reap and get the harvest in. An agreement was first reached between the farmer and the men, then the harvest began in earnest. First the barley was cut with a horse-drawn binder, throwing out the sheaves to be stacked in stooks in neat rows for collecting by the wagons. Then followed the wheat and oats.

The harvesting of the mustard crop was somewhat different. It had to be absolutely dry when formed into wads before they could be gathered and threshed on the field with a steam threshing plant. The mustard was usually grown under contract to Colman's Mustard of Norwich.

Harvest days were long, commencing at 6.30 am and finishing at 7 pm, Monday to Friday, with a 5 pm finish on Saturday. After the binders had finished their role, came the task of carting the sheaves to the stack yards. On a hot summer's day this was an impressive sight, the wagons leaving the yards at a gallop and the men standing with reins in hand, wagons loaded skilfully to a considerable height above the sides. They returned to the stack yard, where the sheaves were stacked in the usual gable-ended style with a 'pitched roof' which, in due course, was thatched. It was noticeable that each yard had its regular stacker supervising the building. Locals could always recognise the handicraft of each stacker; some were better than others, but rarely did the stacks lean over.

After the remaining sheaves were gathered from the fields and the fields raked, they were considered free for the housewives to glean. Prior to the main road arriving, it was quite common to see the ladies across the field, wearing the traditional white bonnets to protect them from the sun, gathering large handfuls of corn and tying the stooks and 'stacking' for collection at the end of the day. This practice was quite common before mainland eggs became available (for most households kept a few chickens). With the arrival of 'Taylor's Dream' the habit changed.

Depending on the weather, harvesting lasted approximately five weeks and the stacks of corn were left to be threshed when the market was most favourable. Before the corn harvest, a period of hay-cutting took place. This was dried on the fields and stacked in the yards and kept in the stack yards until the winter demand. Then men under contract to the mainland buyer would arrive on the scene with the tools of their trade — huge wide-bladed knives about three feet long and extremely sharp. They cut the hay into trusses about 4ft by 2ft, pressing them and binding them to await delivery.

With the coming of the mainland road, the bulk of the farm produce was diverted from the barge to the road and the last vessel sailed from Crouch Loading in 1931, taking some 70 tons of straw from New Wick Farm to London. The straw, in bales weighing about one hundredweight, was loaded by just two men, Mr Clark and Mr Bird.

In the 1930s there were changes in farming. The arrival of the tractor sadly saw the beginning of the end of the handsome Suffolk horses. Science changed the face of farming over the next few years, for corn was produced with a much shorter straw; fertilisers were introduced and the muck-spreading period, so long the joke of comedians, was no more.

More changes were to come, for no longer were white crops to follow black and soon the laying of a field to fallow was a thing of the past.

As war clouds gathered, priority was given to providing food for the nation and combine harvesters appeared. Soon the traditional harvest time was destined for the history books and that annual event of village life was no more. With sheaves disappearing from the fields, commercial farming had arrived. Yet another farming venture was to be seen in the 1930s, for previously peas had been grown, harvested and left in wads to dry. They were now being grown for the canning industry and lorry-loads of women from the east end of Wakering appeared on the fields long before dawn. The object of the early start was soon obvious, for the early dew increased the weight and swelled the pods and, when one realised that such was the speed of the pea pickers that many could pick twenty bags a day, at one shilling a bag, in that period it was big money.

The stack yards then ceased to play any part in the farming year; with an array of rusting implements and empty stables, they looked ghost towns. With all the changes, fewer men were required.

The farm workers on the island were a fine body of independent and highly-respected folk, who daily went about their tasks with a code of self-discipline and a bond of kinship between farmer and employee.

In the late 1920s the Guiver brothers gave up their farms and the tenancies were taken over by Caleb Rayner, from Oldbury Farm in Great Wakering, an astute businessman, who introduced numerous changes. He brought in the Gyrotiller ploughing machine, a huge thing which was manufactured by Fowlers of the Midlands. It was powered by a 150 horsepower engine running at 900rpm and was fitted with a set of Wilders Patch Pole harrows. This machine was first sold for £6,000.

It was first tried on Foulness Island on Monday, 7 November 1932 on the Little Newlands Farm and present at the introduction was Mr Lee, the village policeman, Johnson & Smithers of Fowlers, Spen and George Belton, Caleb Rayner and the operator, Eric Lilley. It did not last many years; maybe the soil was not to its liking. Rayner farmed up to and during the war years. Then he moved on. Perhaps he found the local practices and island farming vastly different from the mainland.

ABOVE: Thirteen horses pulling a hay press along the muddy roads before the coming of the new road. BELOW: Threshing mustard in the field; Fred Webb (the disabled bellringer), Jim Hemstead and Charles Webb snr.

ABOVE: Jack Bird and Jim Rippingale. BELOW: Little
Newlands.

ABOVE: Petter oil engine and threshing machine.
BELOW: Carts at Clark's Hard.

Cutting hay from the stack and BELOW: reaping in the
1920s.

ABOVE: The Gyrotiller. BELOW: Threshing from the stack.

ABOVE: Jack Prailee of Eastwick and 'friend' often barred from the local. BELOW: The Island's prize bullock was on display at Smithfield in 1938 with Alf Shelley.

ABOVE: Steam ploughs. BELOW: Harry Rippingale and
Flacker.

Bill Lilley, eel shearing.

WORK AND PLAY

For a small community, the island made its contribution to the war effort in the first conflict, as sadly evidenced on the memorial. During those years little changed. It was never easy, for a self-contained existence was the order of the day and, apart from a few hardy souls engaged in fishing, the main source of employment was the farms. The fishermen came from the Courtsend village, where Jim Shelley, 'Blinney' Hawkes and 'Bun' Nichols lived. The usual method was to lay down band lines on the sands some miles out to the east, with some thirty baited hooks on each, and to retrieve them after each tide.

The other method was the kiddle system, a large vee-shaped net enclosure staked out on the sand, the catch being gathered at low tide.

Men from the villages frequently made up the crews of the sailing barges plying their trade on the East Coast. Prominent among them were the Ducker families; Gordon Ducker was the skipper of the *Lerline* and the *Violet Syble*. The latter was to finish its days some fifty years later at Salcombe in Devon. Other families connected with the barges were the Webbs, Rippingales and the Hawkes, but by the 1930s islanders ceased to follow this trade, due to the decline in local fleets.

The domestic life of the day was, to say the least, basic; no washing machines or 'fridges, lighting by oil lamp or candle or, if one was fortunate enough, a Tilley lamp which was an advanced form of oil lamp. Electricity did not arrive until World War Two. Much of the limited social life depended on the leadership of the resident vicar and around 1918 that was Reverend Douglas, who followed Reverend Hole. Little was recorded about the latter, except some remember that he had a daughter, known by all as 'Girlie', obviously a young lady before her time.

As well as being sub-standard, homes then lacked most amenities. There were no indoor taps, toilets were at the bottom of the garden, fires were open and the cooking was done on the old black range. A few had Valor Perfection oil stoves. The houses were poorly heated and designed for maximum draught, so nightly retirement to the bedroom was hardly comparable to today's modern central heating. Many folk resorted to a heated fire brick in an old sock at the foot of the bed to combat the cold in the dead of winter.

Most houses had large gardens, no doubt to supplement the weekly wage, but also as a hobby, for the men had few equals in the horticultural field. Coal came from the mainland by barge and cost about £1 per ton in the 1920s. It was supplemented by wood from the usual pile stacked close to the house, the wood having been gathered from the East Coast shore. This was in plentiful supply as wrecks were frequent at that time in the North Sea.

'Shoring' was a way of life on the island, known on the mainland as 'beachcombing', a popular pastime. Some men haunted the sea shores in the early hours, long before dawn, especially after a shorage wind blew up the Turtle Road, Churchend from the south east. There was also an unwritten rule about shoring, that any timber lying on the sea wall was spoken for and that rule was observed by all.

During the Second World War, a Portuguese vessel went down off the east coast of Foulness. Its cargo was many gallons of fine Portuguese wine, much of which came up on the Foulness coastline. Strange to relate, it was the best kept secret of the war, but one can be sure there were many sore heads. Little came to light about this latter-day 'Whisky Galore' episode. One story was told of a local, endeavouring to take home his share. He was in such a sorry state that he stored his bottles in a ditch intending to retrieve them after sobering up. Such was his condition, he was unable to locate the cache and the bottles were never found; at least, no one owned up.

In spite of the peaceful and tranquil surroundings, Foulness had its personal tragedies; in the 1920s and the 1930s, there were several cases of tuberculosis, including my own mother. One family in Churchend even suffered the loss of a father and a teenage son and daughter in a matter of months. Others endured suffering for many years. It was a time when little could be done for them and damp winter conditions hardly helped. History books clearly referred to this when recording the island swamp disease.

Unfortunately, polio also claimed victims. Little was known about it, except that the poor unfortunate victims had to wear a raised boot or use a crutch. Little help was available on the island, but life went on.

Long hours and chores at home left little time for recreation, but the island's two inns provided sources of refuge. There was, however, intense interest in gardening for, apart from their domestic needs, many grew to exhibit in the Annual Show. Such was the fertility of the island, their exhibits were unbeatable.

Soon after the First War ended, Isiah Belton, who farmed the Hall Farm, donated a long wooden army hut to the parish, on condition that it was not to be used on the Sabbath, or for Catholic meetings, Isiah being a strict member of the Baptist faith. It was originally sited next to the Workhouse Yard, which was about a mile due east of the Hall Farm and considered to be about the centre of the island.

However, with the road constructed between the two villages and bypassing the Workhouse Yard, villagers decided to move the Hut to the western end of the field, to the site now occupied by a more modern building. This was done by volunteer labour and the Hut survived until after the Second War.

With the moving of the Hut, a strip was laid for the use of the local cricket club, which moved from the old ground near the Pound, north of the school playing field. It was never first class, as the area was used regularly for grazing, which made the outfield somewhat of a gamble for fielders.

Foulness had a long tradition as a cricket-loving community, an interest no doubt fostered by such enthusiasts as Headmasters Leeds and Miskin, both from Yorkshire and excellent club cricketers. Records show that cricket was played there as far back as the previous century. Foulness sides played regularly around the Dengie Hundred, visiting Burnham on Crouch, Southminster, Bradwell and Paglesham. One wonders how the men got time off to play, especially given the transport difficulties, for it meant travelling by boat to the various clubs across the rivers Crouch and Roach. According to my late father, they worked flexible hours and, with the encouragement of cricket-loving employers, the game thrived and became a way of life.

Over the years the local Burnham paper, edited by the late George Clark, recorded the results of matches played between Foulness and Burnham.

'On May 5th 1913, Burnham scored 136 for seven, declared at home to Foulness, who recorded 41 for nine. Two days later Burnham, with only nine men, reached a total of 89, with the top scorer on 18, Fred Rawlings, on loan from Foulness. The islanders were dismissed for just 37'.

In July 1939, just two months before war began, Foulness were at home to Burnham's Mildmay Iron Works, probably the last match between the old rivals.

Foulness won by one run, after Mildmay batted first. Reg Bradley took four wickets for 12 runs and Buddy Banks and Jim Cook took three each. Playing for Foulness on that memorable occasion were Buddy Banks, Bert Belton, Harry Rippingale, Herb and Ern Potton, R. Bradley, Jake Willsmer, Charlie Hume and Philip Bird. Buddy Banks, Bert Belton and the Potton brothers appear on the photograph of the team in 1914.

With the coming of a road to the mainland, Foulness Cricket Club turned its attention to Southend and District, no longer a sea voyage to the Dengie, but a mere 'bus ride away. It opened a new horizon for the annual fixture list and games at long last against many well known Southend sides.

In the 1920s and 1930s, many of the mainland sides were associated with the local churches, such as Park Road Methodist, St John's, St Mary's of Prittlewell, St Luke's and St Mark's. The teams were well matched and most games were played in the best sporting spirit, but not all. Some incidents were quite unworthy of the ecclesiastical connection; on one occasion, a leading church side refused to accept the umpire's decision. One well known member of the church, Canon Gowing of St Mary's, was not averse to expressing his feelings at the crease with a few well-known adjectives — a popular figure, on and off the field.

One of the most intesting fixtures in the 1930s was against the cricket team of the famous Bryant and Mays' match-making firm, at Snakes Lane, Woodford. It was necessary to leave Foulness early to fit in with the coach firm's schedule, but early starts were nothing new to islanders. The home side beat Foulness.

The island's cricket club survived until some years after the Second World War and many good cricketers have played for it over the years, but regrettably, due to the lack of any form of coaching, they were denied the chance to reach their full potential.

The Hut soon became the centre of village recreation and, among other uses, whist drives were held regularly and a billiard table installed.

The highlight was the Annual Show, on a grand scale and, extremely popular for both residents and visitors. For some outside it became an annual pilgrimage, a meeting of relatives and old friends, but the very success of the Show undoubtedly contributed to its eventual winding-down, as the organisation was completely voluntary and the workload for the highly efficient secretary, Jack Bridge, became too much. Post-war events have been but a shadow of their former glory.

Such was the size of the annual event that several marquees were required, some donated by the War Department which, in that period, adopted a more paternal interest in the daily affairs of the inhabitants than is the case today. There were numerous athletic events, even a 'cycle race where, on one occasion, a man named Hickling appeared in an all-black strip. He was an impressive sight, which added a bit of 'colour' to the main events.

Side shows erected overnight on the side of the Hut did a roaring trade and the crowds enjoyed the pillow fights and the cunning devices to climb the greasy pole, a messy business. Another popular event was throwing the cricket ball, a skill at which locals were adept and which created fierce competition from visiting Burnham men. Some still alive in the 1990s recall local prowess with affection.

Tug-o-war was also a popular event and, on one occasion, the Beltons entered a team comprised solely of members of their family. Pride of place went to exhibits entered by local gardeners, who had few equals, as the Foulness soil was extremely rich and standards high. Enthusiasm was such that many were up long before dawn to get their exhibits on to the show benches. Even the younger generation were not overlooked, with a special class set aside for them for wild flowers, which grew in abundance on the island.

Judging complete, came the grand opening ceremony. On several occasions, the show was opened by commanding officers from Shoebury Garrison, but one year the visiting guest was the British boxing bantamweight champion, Teddy Baldock, who was introduced by Mr 'Sagy' Rawlings, a Foulness man, serving in the Metropolitan Police.

Above all, the Show was a social occasion, a reunion of friends and relatives, although today it is a modest event, still a social gathering, and one of the few days the Ministry of Defence allows free entry to the island. In earlier years, many a Ryder's and Carter trophy adorned local mantlepieces.

Coinciding with the arrival in the 1920s of Reverend Stanton, who was well known as 'the footballing parson', was the formation of the local football team. The game had been played for some years on 'The Skirts' at Courtsend as well as at Churchend. The two villages played each other and on occasions played against a team from Tinkers Lane, now known as New Road, Great Wakering, yet football had never taken off like cricket. However, a side was entered in the Southend and District league and even the parson donned a football shirt. On more than one occasion, his robust play caused an eyebrow or two to rise. The vicar was a man's man, especially when he removed his glasses.

The side gained few honours, but built up a reputation for fair play, with a spirit such that two footballers, Chalk and Miller, travelled from Southend and Ernie Adcock from Great Wakering to play for Foulness.

Locals prominent in the side were Harry Rippingale and George Belton, goalkeepers, and John Belton, a full-back, whose death was due to a tragic gun accident. Also at full-back was Charlie Hume, a ferocious tackler, who was selected to play for the Southend and District side against Southend United at the Kursaal. Others playing for the local side included Reg Bradley, a part-time postman and a skilful player, also Jake Willsmer, who proved he was just as capable with the larger ball. Philip Wheal, who migrated to Wallasea Island, also figured in the team, as did Jack Bird. Alas, a declining population saw the end of the side in the late 1930s.

Foulness recreation and way of life included wildfowling, better known by islands as going to flight, an exercise which required a 12-bore shotgun and a masochistic constitution, sitting for hours waiting for the odd duck or widgeon to come within range. Fortunately for the sportsmen, they were often in abundance on a moonlit night and, apart from their sporting aspect, the birds provided a welcome additon to the daily menu. The sport gave rise to a humorous local comment, from a visit by the local butcher to the home of a Courtsend wildfowler. When asked for her order, the houswife remarked 'no meat this week, "Bun" has shot a plover'. As the plover was one of the smallest wildfowl, one can hardly think she was serious. Was it a hare, the 'forbidden fruit'?

Fishing was also a pastime enjoyed by locals, not with the usual rod and line, but band lines. These were some thirty feet long and at regular intervals had a short line attached, at the end of which was a hook.

During low tide the men would go out on to the Maplin sands to a distance of some two hundred yards and, having located a suitable patch, would then dig for the lugworm. To regulars it was simple; to others it seemed the lugworm knew they were coming.

The worm-baited lines were taken out on to the sands, often as far as the eye could see, and pegged down to await the incoming tide. Those who fished for pleasure walked out to the lines; others who did it for a living often rode across the firm sands on their 'cycles.

The tide having been in and gone, it was time to inspect the lines. Catches were mostly flat fish, such as plaice and flounder, but occasionally in the warm summer months, a silver bass or an eel might figure.

Apart from the joy of fishing, to gaze across the sands on a beautiful summer's morning, to see the sun rise over the golden sand was, by any standard, an exhilarating experience.

Another form of fishing used by the more enterprising was the kiddles, known by the locals as the 'kettles', which comprised a wire mesh or netting, about three feet wide and about one hundred feet long, staked to form a vee at the end of the sea side, with a pocket which trapped the fish going out at the turn of the tide — a simple method, but effective.

Tides had a considerable bearing on the daily lives of early inhabitants for, apart from the use of the Broomway and the shorage winds, it was a source of weather forecasting. The winds would drop with the outgoing tide and the influx of seagulls meant high winds coming.

Leisure as we know it was negligible and, prior to the completion of the main road to the mainland, little was organised. When an event such as a lantern slide display of John Bunyan's *Pilgrim's Progress* was put on, a full house was certain. Such events, prior to the erection of the Hut, took place in the school.

In the early 1920s this was all to change. Before final completion of the road to the mainland, a film show was presented in the village Hut, the first on the island. A silent film, *The Great Train Robbery*, was presented by a Mr Beale, the postmaster from Great Wakering.

It was also in the early 1920s that Jack Taylor, the Government's resident Land Agent and Clerk of Works, endeavoured to relieve the monotony of daily life. He had a marquee erected in his garden adjoining the vicarage and the Dutch bungalow and organised a variety show, featuring Tommy West, a comedian from the mainland. It created immense interest and was remembered for many years.

Naturally, village inns were centres of recreation, or rather the means of escape. The George and Dragon and the King's Head at Courtsend both provided basic drinks. A bar meal consisted of an arrowroot biscuit. They provided a fine venue for local gossip.

As for culture, little existed. There were no library facilities, but several residents set up a self-help project and organised a magazine club, in which each purchased a monthly publication, such as *Punch, Novel,* the *London* and the *Wide World*, which were systematically passed round members. The system worked well.

Winemaking was another thriving hobby, if not an island way of life. Vast quantities were made in huge earthenware containers, with none of the sophisticated methods advocated today, yet there were few failures. Another local pastime was shove-halfpenny, popular in that period, and many a pleasant hour was spent in the garden sheds, under the glare of an oil lamp.

Not all employment on the island was on the farms for, soon after the Great War, the War Department set up a maintenance yard in the Churchend village, commonly known as being 'on check'. In reality it was managed by the Royal Engineers based at Shoeburyness. The site, still evident, was just south of the Hall Farm stack yard and comprised an office, a carpenter's shop and the usual builder's yard, sheds and so on. The works were supervised by a resident Clerk of Works, the first called Hatcher, followed by Jack Taylor who, at the end of the First War, lived in the old Dutch bungalow near the south west corner of the vicarage grounds.

Soon after the completion of the new road, the bungalow was demolished and future clerks were housed in another bungalow on the new development site. Then for a period, the Engineers posted military staff from the ranks of sergeants. Staff Sergeants Rose and

Steward served on the island for a while. Years later, at the end of the Second War, Steward, having become a colonel, returned to the island to serve as a civilian quantity surveyor at a research establishment.

Then a Mr Brownrigg became the resident Clerk of Works and his daughter married Bert Belton. Finally John Bridge, a former plumber, was appointed. He was probably the last of the line.

Among the locals to be employed 'on check', was Bill Dobson, foreman carpenter, bricklayer Harry Ventris, Jack Shelley, bricklayer's labourer, plus Roger Rawlings, the ganger. The seawall gang which took over the responsibility for maintenance when the Government acquired the island, was also based at the yard, although the men spent all their time moving around the wall to the various repair jobs. The gang comprised Did Riley, David Dobson, 'Tally' Nichols and a couple more. In the main, the work of the department was maintenance, a regular job just so long as the money lasted.

At times men were employed from the mainland, but they had to make their own way to the island. The yard survived until the outbreak of World War Two, when the proposed small arms range near Courtsend had to be moved to Wales. The Royal Engineers moved in and it was then called the White City.

The Belton family tug-o-war team.

ABOVE: Show Day: the Beltons. BELOW: Clem Fitch
attending his keddles on the sands.

ABOVE: Foulness Cricket Team 1914: Chas Cater, Basil Dobson, W. Whent, Harry Rippingale, Dick Potton, Bert Belton, Spen Belton, Cecil Ducker, Miskin, Fred Banks, Fred Bush, Ern Potton, Tom Potton. BELOW: The Dutch Cottage, home of the resident engineer in the 1920s.

THOSE IN CHARGE

As with all village life, certain people are destined to play an important role, and so it was on Foulness.

The village policeman, the vicar, the resident Government Agent, the schoolmaster, the district nurse, the customs officer, all were invaluable to the life of the community. All have now left and the island is the poorer for it.

District nurses were a godsend to such isolated communities as Foulness for, prior to the construction of the bridge and road to the mainland, doctors had to travel over the sands along the Broomway. During the Great War, the visiting GP was Dr Roper of Great Wakering and the district nurse up to 1915 was Nurse Smith, who married Spen Belton, son of a local farmer.

Dr Roper used to hire a pony and trap to cross the sands at low tide, a pleasant enough journey in the summer months, but one that could be extremely hazardous in the winter.

Dr Baker, an elderly GP with a surgery in Wakering High Street, took over the role of visiting doctor from Dr Roper. In the mid-1920s Dr Ryan from Shoeburyness, who had a lady partner, Dr Elland, took over the practice, serving the area until the Second World War.

In such a setting, one can appreciate the importance of the village nurse and, after Nurse Smith left, Nurse Bowman arrived and took up residence in a small cottage at the Workhouse Yard with her two small children. Life could never have been easy for her, she was also of the Catholic faith, serving a community who were of a low church environment but, to their credit, the people accepted her as one of their own. She was extremely competent and certainly she had to be, for no doctor was on call at a moment's notice and there was no telephone on the wall. Any emergency could well call for more than is usually required in the line of duty from a district nurse.

Perhaps one incident during her spell on Foulness highlights the importance of her role; it concerns an old character known as 'Hasty', who tried to end it all by cutting his throat. Arriving on the scene, Nurse Bowman threw a bag of flour on to Hasty's throat and he was laid on a bed of straw on a farm cart and taken across the sands to the nearest hospital. He survived the journey across the sands but died later. The incident was described with great relish by Nurse Bowman for many years.

She left the island in the mid-1920s. Her son, Harry, was later to join the RAF and was a fighter pilot in the Battle of Britain, winning the DFC. Unfortunately, he was shot down over the Kent coast and killed. Eileen, her daughter, served with distinction in the nursing profession throughout World War Two in India and South Africa, surviving until 1995.

Nurse Bowman was followed briefly by Nurse Hatch, who then resided in Churchend and finally the village was served by Nurse Lee, the wife of the local constable. Then for a time Nurse Farr was the resident nurse, the last of the line.

Like the nurses, the local constables played an important part in village life, not just keeping the peace, for the island was peaceful enough, but as an essential feature of the community. During the First War and in the early 1920s, the local policeman was PC Reeder, who lived at Bethlehem Row, before moving to Churchend. His successor was PC Lee, who was to be the last of the resident civilian policemen, for the Ministry of Defence took over the role of policing the island, although only in the interests of military needs, civilian duties being carried out by the mainland force.

Constable Lee was a quiet and friendly man, a typical country copper. He fitted admirably into the way of life of the island, a man who religiously carried out his duties regardless of the weather, as a superior officer found out when checking on a bitter winter's night. He found Constable Lee out on patrol regardless. It has to be said it was hardly a rigorous profession, for crime was virtually unknown on the island and no one bothered to lock doors at night.

One misdemeanour is remembered well. On one dark night, while the constable was on his rounds, a girl cyclist ran into him, not equipped with a headlamp, which was not uncommon at the time. The constable was unhurt and, after apologising for being in the way of the 'cycle, the matter was closed.

So the peaceful existence of the local policeman on the island came to an end, to be replaced in the 1930s by the War Department police, in such numbers that some began to wonder if the War Department bred them!

Much of the social life on Foulness depended on the calibre of the local vicar. Rev Hole 1910-1918, was followed by Rev Douglas, 1918-1926. Douglas virtually isolated himself from the bulk of his parishioners and, when by chance they met, he endeavoured to stay aloof, a situation which hardly endeared him to his flock. As for church affairs, his weekly services were of a low church order and were extremely boring.

Little could be said on his behalf and one wonders whatever possessed a man of the cloth to accept a living in such isolated surroundings, yet do so little to help the local residents. A crippled lady residing near the village school relied on being pushed in a wheelchair through the western gate of the churchyard and out through the southern gate, her only means of getting to the village, as the kissing gate was non-negotiable for the chair and the farm gate was on a mud track. For some years, this had been her regular route, until one day the vicar decided to bolt the western gate, preventing the disabled lady from visiting the village. Swift action by a relative, who told Douglas to get the bolt off, or he would smash it off, had the desired result.

After several years the said vicar, according to the Bishop 'had a call', which my late father remarked to the Bishop 'yes, a call of half a crown, instead of two bob' (or two shillings and sixpence instead of two shillings), typical Foulness logic. The Bishop was not amused, but the vicar's leaving caused few regrets. His replacement could not have been more different.

The church of St Mary, Foulness, was an austere building. It was built by public subscription, including large donations from Squire Finch and Trinity House, who gave on condition that the new church had a spire, no doubt an aid to seamen out on the North Sea.

Some eighty years late, the church was suffering from settlement and a contractor was engaged to underpin the main entrance area and also to assist in stabilising the structure. The spire was stripped of its lead sheeting, which was replaced by cedar shingles.

There was a sequel to the spire repairs, for crime arrived on the island, when some mainland 'entrepreneurs' thought they would assist in the disposal of the lead. Arriving by motor cycle and sidecar, they duly loaded the lead, to such an extent that the tyre burst and the stranded thieves were duly apprehended.

In the early post-war years, church policy was low profile, services being held twice on Sunday. Sunday School was also held in both the morning and afternoon, where the youngsters had the fear of the devil instilled in them from an early age. However, the attendances were good. The reward was in the form of attractive religious cards and the right to attend the annual Christmas party and, for a few, a special attendance prize. Services were also held at the St Luke's mission hall at Courtsend.

Low church meant that little of the service was sung and it matched the interior of the church, which has no coloured glass. The whole tone of the church was set by certain church dignitaries and woe betide the housewife who dared to hang out her washing on Sunday, or the youngster who dared to play on the farmer's field.

The call to worship was heralded by a monotonous tone from the single bell. The bell ringer was Mr Fred Webb who, in his early years, had the misfortune to lose his forearm in a farming accident. He was fitted with an artificial arm with a 'Long John Silver' hook at the end. Fred managed quite well by hooking the rope to the hook.

Years later you can still see the grooves in the stone door frame where Fred, not wishing to offend any late-comers from the distant farms, would step outside the porch to see if any of the parishioners from his employer's farm were on their way, while maintaining the chimes.

A major church revolution took place when Douglas left. The church was never the same again. In due course, a new vicar was installed and it was obvious the parochial powers recognised a change was overdue. Reverend Stanton from East London was a complete contrast. In his younger days he had played football at near professional level, was a fair cricketer, above-average billiards player, a good amateur boxer and, as some soon learnt, he could play cards.

Naturally, there had to be changes in the church's affairs, but not without a little local difficulty. Some of the die-hards refused to accept change; some left the church. But Rev Stanton lost no time in implementing change, for he was a born leader. Apart from brightening up the usual services, he recruited members of the church choir, leading from the front, as he had an excellent voice, as well as being an accomplished organist.

At the time, the organ was manually operated and the organists were Dinah Bird (later Mrs Nichols) and Mary Wallace, while the operator managing the pump was a fellow named Bob Manning. There were times when he dozed off, to be awakened by the groan from the organ, much to the delight of the choir. Then one day the organ ground to a halt and, to the amazement of the congregation, an arm, holding a length of wood, shot out from behind the curtain and the voice of Bob could be heard: 'The 'andle's come orf'. Years later, after the Second War and the arrival of mains power, the organ was operated by electricity.

Rev Stanton encouraged a wide range of interests in church affairs and also arranged for numerous visiting preachers. One such was a Mr Pilkington, an aged gentleman who had spent much of his life as a missionary in China. He was said to be the first to actually use the bridge and road, when he travelled all the way from Forest Gate in London on a three-wheeled 'cycle. Fondly known as 'Old Pilk', his life's experiences were an example to all. There were many others who were invited to speak, some better than others, and one well known speaker was Mr Barren, a police court missionary from Shoeburyness.

On Foulness, as befitting a rural community, the harvest festival was the highlight of the year and, come Sunday, the church was packed with fruit, vegetables and farm produce, a colourful display and a pleasant aroma.

78

Combine harvesters had yet to arrive, so sheaves of corn were prominent in the church display and it was one such display about which, it is alleged, Rev Stanton made a comment, regarding the number of thistles in the sheaves. Back came the reply from the farm hand who had delivered them: 'Tell Mr Stanton, the Lord sent both on 'em', delivered in true dialect.

Carol singing in the early 1920s bore little relation to religion or the church. In fact the custom must have been unique to Foulness, for the practice was to recruit a collection of would-be singers and draw up a list of houses to be visited. But there was one proviso, they had be known wine-makers.

Initially, an attempt was made to sing an odd verse or two but, as the night drew on, drink usually overcame song. No money ever changed hands, but next day, many would have welcomed a change of heads. When two local men married mainland sisters the celebrations were held in the Hut and all were invited. Everyone took their fill of the local brew and that night several failed to return home, though several were hardened drinkers. That wine had been stored in wooden casks for just such an occasion.

The arrival of Rev Stanton brought about a drastic change to this annual event, for a more enlightened carol service was arranged, the local church members transported an organ around the village and carols were actually sung. Culture had arrived.

During this period, the church ran what was known as the Girl's Friendly Society, better known as the GFS, but teenagers of that time were somewhat intrigued by this female secret society. There arose a mystery: when did a girl cease to be a girl? Some members seemed to have life membership.

Not to be outdone, their elders had what was known as the Mothers' Union. The vicarage was the centre of village activity and Rev Stanton had the assistance of Len Whent, a local baker's roundsman.

Eventually Rev Stanton decided to move on and left the island in the mid-1930s to take up a parish in Leicestershire. He had played an exceptional role at a time of immense change.

The new vicar was Reverend Marcus Lawrence who, though not so versatile, was a sincere and friendly man and well liked. Tragedy in his personal life made it difficult for him, as a vicar's wife in a village community can be of immense help. However, he had the assistance for a time of a manservant named Leggett and latterly a housekeeper who, incidentally, was the mother of the detective writer, Margery Allingham.

Among visiting tradesmen making casual calls to the island in those days were the various religious bodies known as Corputors, who peddled bibles and religious books. Reverend Lawrence stayed at St Mary's until the Second World War.

Around 1910, Mr and Mrs Miskin arrived at the Church of England School, after a career in Yorkshire. They were assisted by untrained pupil teachers, Miss Riley and Miss Bird, both of whom went on to give valuable service to local education, both on and off the Island.

Miskin was a firm disciplinarian and an advocate of the cane. As for education, it was at its most basic level, beads and shells for counting and slates for writing in the infants' classes. The school consisted of two classrooms, the larger for pupils over eleven years. A playground was set aside for both sexes and had outdoor toilets, which were still in use in 1967.

The senior pupils were taught by Mr Miskin and educational standards seem to have deteriorated. Any child suffering learning difficulties or mental handicap was destined to sit the whole day through with little attention.

Much of the time was spent in what was known as 'free periods' needed, no doubt, to enable the teacher to cope with the mixed classes and age groups. However, in spite of the environment, the attendance records were good. On one occasion, the school won an award for attendance.

Surprisingly, although they were so isolated from the mainland, the children suffered the same ailments. An epidemic of measles, subject to the numbers involved, could mean the closure of the school, until the worst had passed. Anyone suffering from scarlet fever was sent to the isolation hospital in Rochford, on the site now occupied by Purdey's Industrial Estate.

Still, school life had its moments, and diversions in the form of 'art' classes, a misnomer, if ever there was one. These consisted of passing round a collection of black and white cards. Not the slightest instruction was given and children merely had to copy the card to the best of their ability.

Another educational breakthrough materialised when free periods were devoted to the use of the 'Library', which was nothing more than a collection of well-worn books from *The Swiss Family Robinson* to works by Jules Verne and Charles Dickens. The thirst for learning was just as great then as it is today, but opportunities were few.

The school day was from 9am until 3.30pm, except during the long winter nights, when it finished fifteen minutes earlier for, prior to the new road, some of the children travelled up to three miles along a dirt path adjacent to deep ditches which were crossed by single plank bridges, hazardous enough for the older children, let alone infants. It was imperative they should be able to reach their homes before dusk. To their credit, they were seldom absent or late.

School life had virtually no end-product and children had little ambition. There was no point, for it was traditional for the boys to follow father on to the farm and for the girls to enter domestic service on the mainland. As for school amenities, although there was a cloakroom, if children arrived wet, they stayed that way, although on occasions they were permitted to warm themselves by the fire at the end of the classroom. The other fireplace was conveniently placed to warm the backside of the headmaster. There were also occasions in the dead of winter when the children were allowed to eat their sandwiches by the fireside. There were no hot meals provided until the late 1930s.

Like most schools, Foulness Church of England School had its seasons, controlled by no known rules. There were seasons for the peg tops, pitch button, flick cards, as well as the usual boisterous games, such as a line of youngsters facing the wall, bent over behind each other while the rest would run up and pile up on their backs until the line sagged and gave way.

Cricket and football seasons saw the intense rivalry between the two villages reflected on the school playing field, when the weekly game took place between Churchend and Courtsend. It was played in the best sporting traditions and the rivalry on and off the field was always friendly. Each side was chosen under strict residential rules, for an imaginary line was drawn in the region of the Lodge Farm. East of the line were 'Courtsenders', to the west were 'Churchenders', and so it remained. Even when a family moved to a farm across the line, its members remained eligible only to play for the region of their birth.

As for equipment, the education authorities in those days made no contribution towards any sporting activities, so it was a case of self-help and that was achieved by acquiring cast-off gear from the local clubs. This left much to be desired, for the leather footballs had more patches than the original skin and the inners were a mass of John Bull patches. The cricket bats were spliced and bound with twine, the balls of the cork variety, cheap, but adequate. But the games were enjoyed by all.

Exams had little part in the curriculum and the three R's were the order of the day. Being a Church of England School, children were under the watchful eye of the parson, each day beginning with prayers and probably the hymn 'All things bright and beautiful'.

During this period Empire Day was an annual event and the maypole figured prominently in the celebrations, but with he coming of independence for the vast majority of the countries of the Empire, the event ceased to be remembered.

ABOVE: The school and cottages. BELOW: Foulness
Church interior.

ABOVE: Pupils in the mid-1920s. BELOW: Senior Girls
in the 1920s.

Best Days of Your Life

With the departure of the Miskin family in the mid-1920s, the County Education Authority decided in its wisdom, that a nominal roll of a mere sixty pupils did not justify a headmaster and headmistress, so it decided to appoint a mistress and a female assistant.

In due course an aged spinster arrived. Alas, although well qualified, she hardly gave the impression that she would be able to control the situation and so it came to pass. The pupils soon realised the head was, as is often said, a 'soft touch' and they exploited the situation to the full.

It is generally assumed that such actions are the work of some ringleaders, but this was an exception, for every boy seemed to be dedicated to rid the school of what they thought was an affront to their masculinity. In their defence, it has to be said they were the product of the iron fist of the former head, which probably accounted for much of their behaviour. Future years confirmed that view for, when normality returned, as always they were well-behaved.

It was not long after the arrival of the headmistress, Miss Colthup, that chaos reigned and she decided to punish the offenders. The punishment was laughable and treated as a joke, which made the situation worse. It took the form of writing a mere 100 words. Prior to her arrival, the cane ruled. Some soon realised it was possible to write the words in class-time and then hand them in after class; some even had the forethought to do theirs in advance. The girls of St Trinian's had nothing on the pupils of St Mary's Foulness Church of England School.

The headmistress revealed a great new plan. As the classroom was for all ages, she decided the oldest should sit at the front and the juniors at the back. This was followed by a decision to sit boys with girls. It was not clear what she had in mind, but while it certainly did not improve their academic performance, it helped to improve their knowledge of the facts of life. They may have been isolated, but they were no less street-wise than townies.

Incident after incident followed this experiment and, with the senior boys in the front, provided scope for further mischief. The absence of the head for a brief period was sufficient for the clock at the end of the room to be advanced an hour. This was successful on several occasions, until the ruse was rumbled. Although the headmistress made no mention of it, parents were doubtless suspicious of the early arrival home of their offspring, though they never complained. Perhaps they were sympathetic and shared the pupils' feelings.

One of the most outrageous stunts was the importing of field mice into the classroom. They were caught in the nearby Hall Farm stack yard and carried to the school in the boys' pockets, to be released into the vents from the outside. Eventually the mice entered the classroom and rushed around the room, much to the delight of the pupils. The headmistress did not share their enthusiasm.

Not a trick was missed to make her life a misery, such as getting lost in the fog during the morning break. That was a laugh, for the miscreants were country children and it was extremely unlikely that any would really have got lost, even blindfolded. In desperation, the headmistress resorted to corporal punishment. Unfortunately, the culprit refused to put his hand out, so the exercise was abandoned.

In spite of all the unrest, some new ideas were introduced, such as wood-carving, which was popular. However, there was not enough money to buy tools to supplement Miss Colthup's, so it was impossible to continue the subject.

Miss Colthup retired in 1932 and soon the pupils were aware the fun was over. A new headmaster and headmistress were appointed, and discipline was restored.

It was said that the new head asserted his authority by walking between the desks with a cane in his hand and, by all accounts, he knew how to use it. So, in the eyes of the pupils, their action had been vindicated and their self-respect restored and it was thought that never again would a headmistress be appointed to St Mary's Church of England School, Foulness. Alas, it was not to be, for in the years immediately after the Second World War, falling numbers resulted in more drastic changes and pupils accepted the inevitable.

If rules were broken, the damage was slight. None of these children were in trouble in years to come. Several served in the armed forces, in the ranks and at officer level and one even became a Justice of the Peace.

Church choir 1926 — back: Mr Miskin, Rev H. J. Stanton, Bob Manning; centre: John Belton, John Willsmer, Geo Belton, Alf Rawlings; front: Alf Shelley, John Terry, Keith Cater, Percy Nichols, Reg Farr and John Dobson.

ABOVE: The Mill House. BELOW: Wallace's Post Office
and shop.

IN TRADE

In the early years of this century, Foulness had three shops; one was at Churchend, known as the Mill, due to its close proximity to the windmill, which stood some hundred yards to the south until demolished in 1915 and there were two shops at Courtsend.

For some years there had been a weather-boarded shop selling haberdashery and owned by Isiah Belton near the existing boarded cottages in Churchend. Around the time Mr Belton took up farming, he relinquished the shop and the building was demolished in the post-war development programme. It was replaced by a pair of cottages of a more recent design.

The Mill Shop was the main store on the island and was once termed the local Selfridge's, such was the range of goods on sale. It was also the island post office, having the only telephone booth on the island, which was sited in the corner. Included in the black weather-boarded building was the bakery which supplied the whole of the island's needs, bread being delivered by horse and cart. The shop also had a coalyard, which periodically had supplies delivered at the Quay Loading.

The shop was run by Mr Wallace and his three sons and two daughters and in the 1920s and the early 1930s it was a thriving business. Such was the trade, that additional staff were often employed. One of the sons, Ern Wallace, had a small slaughterhouse near the site of the windmill, providing fresh meat for the shop. One of the daughters, Ivy, managed the post office as well as the shop. Goods were supplied wholesale from Enever's of Southend.

The post office was the only link with the mainland in the event of an emergency. It was also the focal point for incoming telegrams, a service frequently used by absent tenant farmers, such as Strutt and Parker, who sent instructions to their resident foreman. The messages were delivered by local youngsters, who were paid a fixed mileage rate. For example, from the post office to Small Gains Farm was ninepence, a princely sum in those days.

Long after closing time, the shop was a popular meeting place for the young men of the village. No doubt the fact that daugher Ivy was an attractive young lady had a lot to do with it. She eventually married the son of the local blacksmith, Alf Dowsett. As for the shop, it was generally accepted that all transactions were cash only, a way of life on the island in a period when no one bothered to lock a door.

The other two shops were at Courtsend, not including the harnessmaker's business at the southern end of the village. One was a small business run by Mr Bird from a house in the northern end of Courtsend, near Blacksmith's Row. When he retired, he handed it over to his son, who continued trading until 1994, when he retired and the business closed.

The other shop was near King's Head and, during the Great War years, was owned by Miss Ballenger. The old building was picturesque, virtually covered in ivy. With the passing of Miss Ballenger, the last of the island Ballengers, the building was demolished and in the redevelopment years, it was replaced with a purpose-built shop on an adjacent site.

The tenancy was taken over by Mr Walter Hawkes, who left the island farms to start a new career. He also took over the twenty acres attached to the King's Head, which he continued to farm for a number of years, when it eventually passed to the neighbouring farmer. The landlord of the King's Head at the time was Mr Whent. Mr Hawkes was a progressive shopkeeper, who endeavoured to stock a wide range of goods, even introducing ice cream to the island.

The shops continued trading until the Second World War, but a declining population and the introduction of the car, meant business fell away. The shop at Courtsend ceased trading and reverted to domestic use. It was also decided to demolish the Mill Shop and transfer shop and post office to No 18 Churchend. So it remains in the 1990s.

There were numerous visiting tradesmen. Among the best known were the Bishops. Perhaps the best known of them was 'Boxey' Bishop and it was not hard to understand why he was no named, for he came to the island from Great Wakering on a 'cycle, which had a carrier both on the front and rear, each with a huge strapped-on leather case. These were packed with household goods, even a few comics for the children. His visits were special, something of a social occasion, for there was none of that high-pressure salesmanship. The unveiling of his wares was done with the same courtesy, whether he made a sale or not.

Another branch of the Bishop family came from Rochford, serving the island from the days when Stanley Bishop and Johnny Bacon made the treacherous journey across the sands *via* the Broomway. They continued their rounds in their pony and trap for some years after the Great War, until declining trade and their own advancing years made them decide to call it a day. Thus ended another chapter of island life. They were highly respected by all the community.

Meat was, to a large extent, home produced, supplemented by the weekly Burnham delivery but, with the coming of the bridge and the road to the mainland, another source of supply arrived. 'Skinner' Shelley of Courtsend, who made a weekly trip in his horse and car to Webb, the Wakering butcher, often arrived home late and delivered after dark. Always a welcome visitor, 'Skinner' was often partial to a 'refeshment' stop.

Apart from the regular visiting tradesmen, several others attempted to build up a business connection with the households, for in the early 1920s Foulness was, to the outside world, something of an uncharted area and its potential market an unknown factor. For a brief period, Pipe, the bakers of Shoeburyness, attempted to establish themselves and their fancy cakes were a welcome change, but they found it was not viable.

Then a fish and chip van arrived on the scene, only to catch fire *en route;* it was never seen again. For a short period, a family from Tinker's Lane, Great Wakering sought to establish a greengrocery round, but Foulness was hardly fertile ground for such a venture and the visits ceased. One business was successful. Mr Stowe, also from Great Wakering, built up a Sunday connection with his paper round.

Walter Hawke's shop at Courtsend.

91

ABOVE: Children on BELOW: Crouch Corner beach.

A CHILDRENS' PARADISE

No children had a more idyllic life than those who lived on Foulness, for they were as free as the birds and the days were all too short. This was before Government restrictions, introduced in the early 1930s. In the previous decade children were allowed to wander at will all over the island and they took advantage and enjoyed it to the full.

Farmyards, fields and ditches were open to all and, although the winter nights might be extremely harsh, they were followed by warm summer days. Even the short winter days had their attraction, for the hard frosts froze the ponds and a winter sports ground was available free. Many of the ponds in the 1920s were considerably larger than they are today.

To youngsters of those far-off days, the seawalls were the Mecca of their generation, a veritable pleasure ground, an area of adventure. Often on Saturday mornings they would set off with a few sandwiches to tide them over until returning home, to spend a few hours on the eastern wall and the saltings for, just as it was for their elders, the saltings seemed to lure youthful adventurers. This was an area where it was safe for the children for, while it could be a treacherous journey over the sands *via* the Broomway, many tides hardly covered the saltings.

It was a fascinating area, quiet beyond belief, broken only by the abundant birdlife walking on the flat sand. When the tide was out on a sunny day, one could see miles of sand glittering in the light and perhaps a cargo vessel in the distant North Sea. On the western side of the island, it was a different story, for the waters were deep, so it was an unwritten rule that the rivers were out of bounds to the young. It was surprising, but few children could swim. The residents of Courtsend used to go the Weir Corner area, which had a small shell beach. Some enjoyed a swim and a member of the Bird family actually swam with a pipe in his mouth.

The saltings were the main source of adventure for the children, a chance to explore the numerous miniature creeks to search for marine life and the flotsam which came ashore with each incoming tide. At low water, countless treasures from the North Sea could be revealed, such as the numerous matchboxes washed up from passing ships. Adventurous minds immediately turned to foreign lands, the obvious source of those boxes.

This was juvenile 'shoring' at its best; for every lad was well versed and a keen student of the tides. They, like their elders, observed the unwritten rule, that any object, such as timber, left on the seawall, was claimed property.

Most youngsters of the day owned what was called, in the local dialect, a 'storn shurter', or in the King's English, a stone shooter, better known on the mainland as a catapult. The youth of the period was quite expert in the use of this weapon and perhaps not always lawfully, for visits to the seawall enabled experts to get in some useful practice, targeting the telephone insulators on the lines, which went along the poles around the walls for military use. Even in that peaceful setting 'boys will be boys'.

Birdnesting featured prominently in the life of youngsters, for Foulness had an abundance of birdlife, some rarely seen elsewhere, such as the kingfisher, the coot and the heron, which haunted the reeded ponds, a sure sign there were fish in the vicinity. All the birdlife of Britain seemed to haunt the island, an ideal environment, and the survival rate was high. Even the deep ditches added to the spice of life, where eels were numerous and their presence detected by a black ring in the mud; they could be caught by using an eel shear, a long pole with prongs at the end. The banks were also the hiding place of the water rat. Although quite harmless, they were fair game for youthful hunters.

It was an ideal era for children, an island waiting to be explored. Every tree was climbed, although there were few established ones on the island and one area was particularly prominent in the life of the Churchend children. It was the area known as Round Gardens, about 200 yards north of the Mill Shop. It comprised a raised mound, surrounded at times by water. In the garden was a huge elm tree, as well as numerous tamarisk trees and a variety of shrubs.

This was a safe area for chldren and countless hours were spent in this miniature island paradise, the youngsters' very own, handed down from generations past. Yet in the years following the Second War, the whole area was levelled, on the excuse that there was a need for greater food production. This destroyed a valuable part of the islands' heritage, sadly with not a voice raised in protest.

There were, during that period, several derelict sites, such as Bethlehem Row, where there had been an old blacksmith's forge. This was another source of pleasure for the young and an added bonus was the fruit from the existing trees still flourishing around the ruins.

Foulness also had its beaches, small, but popular with families. One, the shell beach at Crouch Corner, was a delightful haven of rest, completely unspoilt and, as a bonus, it had the wreck of the *Donus* beached on the shells. This wreck gave countless hours of enjoyment. Years later, it finally succumbed to the northerly gale.

The other beach was at Weir Corner, north east of Courtsend. This was also an unspoilt shell beach and popular with Courtsend residents.

Pocket money is cherished by all children, but on the island there were many ways of raising a copper or two, such as at harvest time. There the youngsters often assisted in the fields and behind the carts during mustard threshing, gleaning the left-overs. Another Saturday morning job was pulling the docks out of the crops and then there was the pleasant task of acting as beaters for a visiting shooting party.

Yet the money earned still never seemed sufficient for, although there were no high-pressure salesmen or television adverts, there were many more subtle inducements, such as the small sticks of rock sold at the Mill Shop. About one in every fifty had a streak down the centre that entitled the purchaser to a free stick.

On the island, as on the mainland, there were collectors of cigarette cards. The leading brands of cigarettes included cards of top sporting personalities. Capstan cigarettes had cards of superior quality and are now collector's items, so it was quite usual to hear the cry as the smoker left the shop: 'got any fag cards?'.

Some enthusiastic youngsters endeavoured to supplement their pocket money by trapping the moles which frequented the lucerne fields. The technique was to set a spring mole trap near a ditch. This could yield a daily catch, which entailed a morning visit from the youthful trapper before going off to school. The moles were skinned and dried out, then posted to a firm in East London known as Brudneys, which sent back a postal order for sixpence a skin. One wonders at the reaction of the firm had it known with whom it was dealing. Perhaps it knew — and it treated our 'trappers' fairly.

November the fifth, Guy Fawkes's Day, saw the island youngsters celebrating in a somewhat different manner than is the custom today. On this memorable occasion, children dressed up for the event with suitable masks, then after dark the boys would tour for some miles around the farms and cottages of the villages, knocking on the doors after reciting doggerel known as 'The Cobs', a burlesque verse of no known origin.

The Cobs

Remember, remember, the fifth of November
The Gunpowder Treason and Plot
I should like to know the reason
Why the Gunpowder Treason should ever be forgot
For this is the night, that he would strike,
To blow the King's Houses of Parliament up alive.

Three score barrel and six below
To cause Old England's overthrow
By God's mercy he got caught
With his dark shadow and lighted torch
Shout boys, shout boys, make your voices ring
Hollah boys hollah boys,
God save the King!

Finally, the ritual completed, the householder would invite them in and endeavour to identify the callers. It was a good-natured event and concluded with perhaps a mince pie and a few coppers.

If the children were not literally streetwise for, apart from the main road, there were no streets, they were well-versed in the farming year, they were students of local affairs and they kept a watchful eye on the well-kept stack yards, for therein lay the source of rich pickings, the mouse.

They were well aware that, if the stacks were threshed before Christmas, the mice would be in short supply, but come Easter, it was an entirely different state of affairs, as the stacks would be teeming with them. So, when the steam engines arrived at the wheat stacks with their threshing tackle, it was 'let battle commence' and the farm hands steadily fed the sheaves into the machine and slowly reduced the stack to a manageable level for the youngsters. who appeared on the scene during lunchtime.

Mice poured out of the stack and were hit with sticks by the surrounding youngers, who hastily stored their victims in tins or in their pockets, a practice not exactly condoned by their parents, as their offspring thereafter smelt like a farmyard. That did not deter the island's young entrepreneurs, who carefully stacked the mice so that, at the end of the day, Mr Belton paid them one penny per score. The count could exceed thousands. The count was done by the youngsters and the result was never questioned.

Sadly, with the coming of the combine harvester, that pleasure was lost for all time, no doubt to the relief of all parents.

Foulness youngsters also enjoyed the more traditional forms of entertainment for, like their elders, they loved a game of cricket. Indeed, they played on any available flat grassland and, unlike their counterparts on the mainland, they did not have to seek permission to do so. Games were even played in the moonlight on the new road and on occasions, the wickets were pitched on the fields. That certainly gave the batsmen a taste of spin.

Few children had a better lifestyle than those on Foulness Island, a truly idyllic juvenile setting.

ABOVE: Dobson family at Crouch Corner. BELOW:
Maplin Sands and the Saltings.

Isiah Belton.

SONS OF THE SOIL

In spite of the isolation of Foulness, over the years the inhabitants have always had ambitions to improve their lot, whether on the island or in far-off lands. Some made up the crews on the barges that plied their trade up and down the rivers and the neighbouring coastline, some served in the public services in the City.

Then again, some sought to make their fortunes in far-off lands, like Jack Rippingale who, with a colleague, migrated to Oak Bank, near Winniipeg in Canada. He virtually started from scratch and became a successful and well-known business man. He changed from arable farming to bee-keeping. Such was his success that he was called upon to lecture on the subject in the United States. He was also successful in the real estate business. Some years later, he was joined by members of the Whent family, of the King's Head Inn. Descendants of the Whent family still reside in Canada.

In the post-Great War years, there was a man named Len Whent, a rather pale and frail man said to be an asthma sufferer, yet a keen athlete. He was also a dedicated churchman.

His working life was as a baker's roundsman, employed by the Wallace family at the Mill bakery and daily he could be seen dashing around the cottages or on the cart, delivering to the outlying cottages. During the 1920s and 1930s, Len played a prominent part in the affairs of the island's church, becoming a registered lay preacher. It was during those years he was encouraged by both Rev Stanton and Rev Lawrence.

Then in 1939, having been ordained, he migrated to Western Australia, as part of the Big Brother movement. Some time after the outbreak of war, he joined the 31/51st Australian Infantry Battalion as a chaplain, serving in Dutch New Guinea, often taking part in patrols into the interior. Later he embarked for Bouganville, where he shared with the troops the rigours and hardships of the campaign that followed, often putting his life at risk as he moved in the forward areas to carry out his ministry.

After 27 years of service in Western Australia, Len was appointed a Canon by the Bishop of Bunbury. He passed away in 1986 at the age of 82.

Foulness can rightly call Len one of its own, although it was a far cry from his humble beginnings at the King's Head Inn at Courtsend to the vast area of Western Australia.

The Belton family is part of the story of the island. Early in the twentieth century, Isiah Belton took over the old shop and, after purchase, still peddled goods around the islands and over on to Burnham marshes. He was described as a pedlar on his son's birth certificate. Such ventures meant the use of a rowing boat. The old weather-boarded shop was next to the existing boarded terraced row at Churchend, and was demolished in the early 1920s.

Isiah was an extraordinary man by any standards. He never received any formal education and was largely self-taught. He never went to the Foulness church, being of the Baptist faith and it was said he declined to have his youngest son christened at St Mary's. Nevertheless, he was well-respected on the island.

There were four sons: George, Spen, Hube and Bert. The older three were all married on the same day in 1910 and the whole island was invited to the reception in a Hall Farm barn. Initially George lived in Hall Farm and Isiah stayed in the shop until it was demolished. Then, with the erection of a house designed as a farmhouse in the village, George moved into No 18 Churchend and Mr Belton senior moved into the Hall. Then Isiah Belton decided that it was not practical to have all his sons on the island, so Hube moved on to Sheepcotes Farm in Hockley, where he farmed for some years.

Many years later, Mrs Hube Belton, née Dobson, used to describe her experiences in the years prior to the erection of the bridge; how she drove a pony and trap from Hockley and crossed the sands single-handed. If the tides were against her, she stopped the night at the Anchor in Great Wakering.

Spen started his farming career at Eastwick Farm but, after the tragic loss of his wife, he moved to Great Hayes and later to Stewards Elm Farm in Stambridge.

Hube eventually turned his hand to development, building four bungalows and two houses in Brays Lane, Rochford. Never a man afraid to venture upon a new career, he turned to shopkeeping, for in the late 1920s he purchased a general store in West Road, Shoeburyness, which comprised a butcher's, grocery and coal merchant. He traded until the end of the war, selling out to the Co-op, but he always retained his love of the soil and cattle dealing, being the 'offshore' agent for the Foulness farms.

Many stories have been told about Hube and his exploits, which started from the days when he was engaged at an early age in horse-dealing, and during the First War, he was asked by the Army to purchase horses. It was said on his first venture in cattle dealing, an old man remarked 'You're young, do you know what to look for?' Hube replied 'Yes, I think so'. 'Good lad, but let me give you a word of warning, beware of the man with the Bible under his arm, he'll be the one to catch you.'

Hube was never a man to stand on ceremony or to worry about dress. In the early 1920s, when he and his colleagues were passing through London from some cattle-dealing exercise, still in their working clothes and, with an aroma to match, the party called at a fashionable hotel, to be told it catered only for the best type of people. Hube replied 'That'll do for me' and pushed past the astonished doorman.

The mid-1920s saw Hube in a new career, as a general storekeeper in Shoeburyness. One incident happened during the war years, when Hube suspected he was the victim of shoplifting. There were no cameras in those days, so he set about trapping the thief by tying a string to a pound of butter. In due course the thief was caught.

Then in the 1930s, the Cater families, who farmed the Naze Wick and Lodge Farms, relinquished their tenancies and the farms were taken over by the Belton family. Spen moved into the Lodge and the Beltons became the largest farmers on the island.

In this period, Isiah lived in the Hall Farm house and Bert, the youngest son, recently married, moved into the cottage next door, which was originally termed the Mens' Kitchen for, like most farms on the island, there were quarters set aside for itinerant workers and local men who were forced to leave crowded households. Many of the cottages on the island were too small to cope with the usual large families.

In his advanced years, Isiah was still a finely-built man with a flowing white beard and was often to be seen in the Hall Farm stackyard, with a long stock whip in his hand. Youngsters roaming around the yard gave the old man a wide berth, not that there was ever any need, for he was kindly and many benefited from his generous nature. A God-fearing man, Foulness owes Isiah Belton a debt of gratitude, in more ways than one.

The Guivers were resident on the island for some sixty years and held tenancies on several farms, as well as being the licensees of the George and Dragon Inn. The family consisted of Bert, Harry and Philip, who died at an early age. As well as the brothers, a sister, named Cissie, lived with them.

According to local legend, anyone standing outside the main door of the Foulness Church at midnight on Hallowe'en night, would witness all the funeral processions for the forthcoming year.

It was said that Philip, who did not enjoy the best of health, stood outside the door on one such night and saw a funeral of his own family going by, noticing that all the family were present, except himself. He died during the coming year, as the legend implied, and he was buried near the main church door.

The Guivers were a reserved and respected family and known as caring employers. A typical example was their employment of Bob Manning as a general hand around the inn, responsible for the milking of the small dairy herd, which was taken down daily to the Glebe meadow for grazing. It was said the Guivers were the only suppliers of fresh milk on the island.

Bob was a simple fellow, so regular employment was welcome; the family protected Bob, to such an extent that, if anyone called at the pub at midday and asked for Bob, the brothers would invariably reply that he was not to be disturbed until he had had his midday nap.

Bob had learnt over the years that, if he failed to milk the cows dry, they would dry earlier and so it came to pass that each year milk ran out earlier than the average at the Dragon.

The brothers were always immaculately dressed with high-polished leather gaiters, typical of country gentlemen. It was generally considered they were of independent means, to whom farming was, in many ways, a hobby. At the George and Dragon, at times they went out of their way to avoid custom. One show day in the 1930s, when visitors from the showground packed into the pub, one of the customers remarked 'Not enough seats, Harry'; back came the reply 'Enough seats, too many backsides'.

Regrettably at times, tragedy goes hand in hand with a comfortable lifestyle, for living with the family for a period was a relative called Sam Meen. Poor Sam decided to end it all with a shotgun at a time when suicide was considered a mortal sin. Like others, he was laid to rest in unconsecrated ground near the western end of the church, next to the graves of unknown seamen washed up on the shores.

In the late 1920s, the Guiver family relinquished the farming side of their business, but continued in the George and Dragon until the Second World War. They retired in the 1940s after a long and distinguished vocation extending over sixty years. The late shopkeeper at Courtsend, Miss Louise Ballenger, was a cousin, as were the Belchams, who farmed Priestwood Farm for a time. Roy Belcham, a relation of the well-known branch of the family in Southend, was a familiar figure in the village, as was Miss Tomlin, who frequently stayed at the inn.

Arthur Shelley, the son of 'Wick', resided at the Quay Farm and was severely disabled, partially paralysed and deformed, which was probably the result of an early case of polio. But he was determined to make the best of life and learnt shoe-repairing, which provided a modest living. He also acquired a 'cycle, specilly adapted for his needs.

Not to be outdone, like the rest of his contemporaries, he was a devout lover of cricket and was accepted as a valuable member of the Foulness Cricket Club, being the regular umpire, standing at the wicket, leaning on his crutch. Few challenged his knowledge of the game. World War Two gave Arthur the opportunity to join the labour market in the national war effort and he left the island to take up employment in Chelmsford. He later married and lived to an advanced age.

Mick O'Keefe was not a local-born celebrity, but a colourful fellow nonetheless. Much of English village life is built around its local characters; Mick was just such a one.

He must have arrived on the island some time around the beginning of the First War. Locals used to say he was shipped over from his native Ireland with a herd of cattle, as they could not tell the difference.

However, Mick endeavoured to integrate into island life and married a local girl. From then on it was obvious he was alert to any form of progress for, when the new road was opened, Mick saw the possibility of tourist trade, selling teas. That was short-lived, because the War Department restricted entry to the general public in the early 1930s.

Mick also took up bee-keeping, alas with mixed fortunes. Complaints were made about the condition of his honey, for hairs were found in it. Mick hotly disputed this in his Irish brogue; he could not understand how this could happen for he had strained it through a sandbag.

With the arrival of motorcycles, Mick was to the forefront, acquiring a belt-driven Enfield, thus enabling him to attend Southend United football matches at the Kursaal. Every Saturday he set off with Alice on the pillion. Legend has it that, on one occasion, Mick arrived at the Kursaal minus Alice, thought to have fallen off *en route*.

Finally, Mick's past caught up with him for, when the War Department set up the Royal Engineers' yard at Churchend, unofficially known as 'on check', he obtained work as a labourer, but the age he gave then did not match the age he claimed when reaching retirement. He had forgotten that the date of birth he had given when starting with the Royal Engineers was incorrect. So much to his disgust, he was forthwith retired.

For many years, Mr Threadgold and his son had been in business as the Courtsend blacksmiths in Blacksmith Row at the northern end of the village. The business differed from that run by Mr Dowsett in Churchend, for it was mainly a farriery, which thrived until the arrival of the tractor and the end of horses in the 1930s. The business closed and the family purchased a farm known as

Oxenhams, near Rushley Island in the Havengore Creek, still farmed by the family in the 1990s.

Frank, the only son, was a prominent sportsman in the district, an accomplished footballer as well as a distance runner in the Southend area. He was married to Eve Hume, a member of the well-known Hume family, who resided at the New Wick farm.

The Mannings lived in a small, semi-detached house among a row of houses known as Smokey Cottages, near the Quay Farm. They were a harmless, lovable collection of brothers and sisters. There were two sisters; Jane, who virtually ruled the household and, with such a small house, it was certainly neded, and Alice. There were six brothers. The eldest was 'Tubby', who had seen service in the Great War and was invalided out of the Army. He was the proud owner of a pony and trap. The pony was stabled in a shack on the banks of a nearby ditch. In spite of some difficulty in walking, Tubby got around the island and regularly made it to the post office to collect his 'Lloyd George', as the state pension was known.

Stories abounded about Tubby. One, often repeated, was the occasion when he purchased a return rail ticket and then, not using the return half, proudly boasted that he had 'done the old railway'! One relates when Tubby was due for an appointment in London, to be reassessed for his war pension. He set off across the wet and muddy fields, managing to fall over on numerous occasions before boarding the train. He duly arrived before the medical board looking an appalling sight. Such was his condition that he was never asked to appear again.

Billy, some years younger, set out to make his mark in the community, for he purchased a cockle bawley from a yard in Paglesham and surprised the vendor by presenting the cash for the boat in a biscuit tin. Billy also purchased a Rudge motorcycle, which was the super-bike of the 1920s. Not that Billy sailed far, or covered much in the way of mileage, but he derived immense pleasure from simple ownership.

'Affie', around Billy's age, worked at the Shelford farm. He too was the proud owner of a motorcycle. Unfortunately, Affie built up a reputation for malingering and was, in his later years, often off sick. One assumes he was a member of the slate club, to which most men on the island belonged. Members received a modest weekly payment when off sick and naturally others kept a watching brief on all the claimants, for at the end of the year, any surplus was paid out to the members. No doubt Affie's record was duly noted, but his reputation proved unjust, for he had been suffering from a long-term injury and finally died in middle age.

One of the older brothers was Ike, an eccentric who worked on a local farm. He was always the butt of village children, who delighted in dashing across in front of him when he rode along he village path, crouched over his semi-dropped handlebars. On his regular ride to work, when he rode along the footpath close to the vicarage grounds around 6am, he could be heard muttering 'It's orlright for that bloody owd parson', for the parson was still in bed.

The other brothers included 'Dampon', who worked on the farms and the youngest, Bob, who worked at the George and Dragon.

The jewel in the crown of the Manning family was Eric, the son of a daughter working on the mainland. He was in the care of uncles and aunts. Eric was, in many ways, a truly remarkable fellow. He certainly did not receive much stimulation from the rest of the family in Smokey Cottage, yet it soon became obvious he was gifted. His first employment was on a local farm, which he disliked immensely. Fortunately, my late father found employment for him as a trainee carpenter on the Royal Engineers' Depot and there he stayed until service regulations required his resignation. Jobs there were normally reserved for ex-servicemen, and those who had not served were the first to be put off in slack times.

His career then took him to the mainland and eventually to London. Alas, tragedy struck and Eric lost his wife after a long illness. Years later he also lost his daughter and son-in-law, but he was one of those rare individuals who could smile in the face of adversity. Not only was he of a happy disposition, he had an excellent tenor voice, was handsome and had a flair for entertaining others.

Finally, following a career with the Rochford Rural District Council as Clerk of Works, Eric left England in 1979 to join his son in Queensland, Australia, but even then bad luck followed him as he was afflicted with Parkinson's disease. He spent several happy years in his own bungalow near Ipswich, Queensland, as popular as ever, entertaining new-found friends. He still kept in touch with the old country and his sixteen-page letters were a joy to read, if written with great difficulty.

A visit to the Manning household was always an enjoyable experience, welcomed by 'Come in boy!'. They were an unforgettable family.

One of the best known farming families on the island were the Caters, farming Naze Wick, where Charles resided and the Lodge Farm, home of Walter Cater. Both were devoted members of the church, Walter regularly attending sevices, driving there in his pony and trap. Charles Cater was, for many years, a keen supporter of the local cricket team.

Like the Belton brothers, the Caters were breeders of Shire and Suffolk horses. Charles had one son, Charles junior, who was educated at a private school in Southend, where he had the benefit of a qualified cricket coach and subsequently became an able local cricketer.

Shortly before the Second World War, the farms were handed over to the Belton family and Charles junior declined an offer to continue at Naze Wick, obtaining work in the Ministry of Defence, and leaving the island.

Walter Cater had one son, named Keith, who was disabled. Initially he was educated at the vicarage and later at Clark's College. Keith was partially paralysed, but that did not deter him from enjoying a game of cricket. He eventually left the island and lived in the north of England after the war years.

Another brother, Jack Cater, was well known in the Rochford area, farming at Scotts Hall, near Canewdon. He too was a cricket lover, having his own private ground.

In the village of Churchend lived an old lady known as Molly Cater well remembered by an elderly Burnham resident in 1994. Once described as 't'owd witch', she was really a friendly eccentric.

Intinerant farm works were regular visitors to the island during the summer months, living in the mens' kitchens. Jack Prailee was one and he and his opposite number, Joby, who lived at Eastwick, were conspicuous in more ways than one. Jack's love of beer eventually led to his being barred from the George and Dragon. Both were not averse to eating maggot-infested cheese.

Also in Churchend in the 1920s was Mrs 'Ginger' Hempsted, a lady who kept her own counsel, but every mid-day visited the George and Dragon, long skirts flowing and head held high, with a bottle in a bag, *en route* to the front door of the pub to collect her beer. This was the occasion for the daily ritual of village curtains drawn back by unseen residents, but who could deny her her pleasure? She had had more than her share of tragedy. She was the stepdaughter of Jimmy Dowsett.

Probably the best known character of the period was Phoebe Webb, who resided in Churchend, in the same house all her life. She passed away in 1994 in her late 80s. She was a typical Foulness Islander, with a strong 'Foulnessian' accent, and a memory second to none. Visiting scribes made her their number one source of information. A spinster, she had lived and worked all her life on Foulness.

Perhaps 'Jummy' Shelley was a classic example of the way of life on the island for, in his 94th year, he purchased a new graft. Jummy lived at Courtsend near the harness makers and he had a large garden. Like all islanders, he planned to dig the heavy Foulness soil in the autumn, to allow nature's frosts to break down the clods. A graft was ideal for the job. It is longer than the normal garden spade, with the steel blade designed straight from the wooden shaft, giving extra strength. Alas, Jummy did not survive long after his purchase, but his attitude was typical — resilient, lively and hopeful.

As time passes and memory dims, others may have been overlooked, for few remain to recall that decade. In the immortal words of the late Charles Cater, 'Poor owd boys, orl gorn, orl gorn'.

'Last of the Foulness Summer Wine' — Tubby Manning, Billy Manning, David Dobson, 'Wadger' Webb and Shin jnr.

ABOVE: Will Whent (brother of L. G. Whent, Australia),
Eva Whent (née Boosey), Jack & Mrs Rippingale at
Oakbank, near Winnipeg, Canada in the 1920s. BELOW:
Cutting the churchyard: Jim Farr, Walter Farr, Fred Bush
and 'David' Dobson.

EPILOGUE

1939, and war is declared. Foulness, as was expected, played its part in the war effort, both in a military role and in the drive for increased food production. The island also had its own Home Guard. With the evacuation of the Small Arms Establishment to South Wales, the 'White City' near Courtsend became the centre for anti-tank trials and other areas were used for artillery ranges.

After the cessation of hostilities, several new houses were erected, both in Churchend and Courtsend, but they were outnumbered by the number demolished.

In the late 1940s, the Ministry of Defence ring-fenced the farms at Shelford, Smallgains and New Marsh to accommodate a vast top security research establishment. Initially it was the Armament Research Establishment (ARE) and the High Explosives Research Establishment (HER), the parent station being at Fort Halsted. Then in the 1950s, the establishment was taken over by the United Kingdon Atomic Energy Authority and the ARE moved to Potton Island. The establishment was under the authority of Aldermaston, Berkshire.

The UKAEA Foulness was a completely self-contained unit, with trial ranges, administration block, a surgery, cinema and lecture theatre, library, a licensed canteen, workshops and laboratories, as well as a successful apprentice school. During the cold war several hundreds were employed, then with improved relations with the eastern block, numbers steadily declined.

In the 1970s, the Establishment reverted back to the Ministry of Defence and finally became known as the AWE.

A further establishment was built near Clark's Hard, due west of Naze Wick farm. It is known as the Environmental Testing Establishment (ETC), a much smaller unit, which is still in existence in 1996.

Most of the 7,000 acres are still devoted to agriculture, farmed by two farmers: Burroughs, who came from the Hanningfield area in the 1940s and the Beltons, no longer Belton Bros, but Belton Farms.

1953 was an epic period in the history of the island, when the North Sea once again invaded. Yet again the islanders had to leave their homes, several never to return. This time the Broomway was no longer a perilous journey, as the Army came to the rescue, using amphibious vehicles.

Returning to the island as the water receded was an eerie experience for, as the sun shone on the drying land, it was as though

109

nature had deserted the island. There was complete silence and not a sign or song of a bird, an environment devoid of any living creatures. But the land soon recovered, helped by a treatment of gypsum. The landscape had changed little and any loss of the island's trees was replaced by a modest tree-planting scheme.

The late 1960s saw Foulness once again facing change, with the proposal to site the Third London Airport on its shores, to be known as Maplin Airport. With a change of government, the project was shelved.

So what of today's Islanders? Having been privileged to work with many of my former island colleagues, I found nothing had changed; they are still as reliable and dedicated as their forefathers. Life on the island was changing rapidly in the post-war years and the declining numbers at the small school presented a problem. The first decision was to transport all the senior pupils to the mainland and to keep the Church of England school open for juniors but, when the roll call amounted to a mere fiften, the school closed in 1988. After some 140 years, junior pupils now travel daily to Great Wakering.

During those years, many teachers served the educational needs of the island, none more so than Miss M. Wolsencroft, who was head teacher for 29 years, and who, with dedicated assistants, achieved remarkable success for such a small school in such an isolated environment. Like their predecessors, the post-war generation took full advantage of the opportunities available to them, all arising from Taylor's Dream.

In the academic field, some achievements were quite remarkable, for a generation whose ancestors were described as 'Sons of the Soil'.

Timothy Webb, BSc, Birmingham University, is now employed at GCHQ, Cheltenham; Trevor Willsmer, a former apprentice with AWRE, gained a Civil Engineering degree at Birmingham University, worked as an engineer in Zambia, and is now a Chief Engineer at Port Hedland in Western Australia.

Mrs Pamela Bridge, née Dobson, graduated from the London University with a degree in French and German and took up a post with Barclay's International in the City of London, while Gillian Farr studied Drama at the Huddersfield Polytechnic, obtaining a BA. She then trained at the Old Vic in Bristol and is now employed by the BBC; Nicholas Farr graduated from Sussex University, with a BSc and is now employed in accountancy.

Now in 1996, Foulness Island is still as isolated as ever, no longer by the natural environment, but by the needs of the defence industry and security restrictions. With the ending of the cold war and the cut-back in military needs, one can but wonder if the isolation is really necessary.

The population has fallen to around 200, now centred in the two villages. There is just one shop, which includes the Post Office, which is in Churchend. The King's Head pulled its last pint in the 1980s. John Nichols was the last licensee, having taken over from Mr Cook after the floods of 1953. Sadly, another part of the island's heritage has gone for, with undue haste, the Ministry of Defence demolished the outbuilding which held the licensed premises, a classic case of Ministerial vandalism, leaving just the George and Dragon at Churchend.

Surely the island has reached crisis point — a far cry from Taylor's Dream of the 1920s.

The school stands empty and the house is let to an ex-teacher. There is no resident vicar and the vicarage is let to a tenant. The Church still stands, majestically towering above the flat land, as austere as ever with not a single stained-glass window. Yet the interior is meticulously maintained by a few of the devoted, ever-dwindling number of parishioners. The polished wooden pews gleam in the sunlight, just as they did when the author was a boy.

Nothing seems to have changed, although the organ is electrically pumped and the lighting is from the mains. A closer look at the organ gives rise to just another of the island mysteries, for there is attached a polished brass plate, bearing the following inscription: 'This organ was built in 1868, obtained a gold medal at an exhibition, purchased from Ockendon Parish and dedicated on March 10th 1908, to commemorate King George V's Silver Jubilee in 1935'.

Services are still held in St Mary's, conducted by the vicar of Great Wakering, who now administers to the needs of the two parishes, but it is an uphill struggle, for the churchyard is a scene of utter neglect. Why, one may ask, should it be so? The Ministry is the landlord, acting as the twentieth century squire. It restricts visitors from maintaining the graves of their ancestors, should they wish to do so. Surely under such circumstances there is a moral obligation to assist the community, as the defence people would have done in earlier years.

Recently, the churchyard has been declared nearly full, causing some local concern, as it was feared that future interment would have to be on the mainland. But land was acquired, at considerable expense, a burden to be borne by the few. The previous extension to the burial ground was achieved by merely moving the fence. Alas, times *have* changed.

Today the whole way of life has changed. The farms no longer need the farmhand as in the past, and the 'RE Yard', now at the

'White City', west of Courtsend, is but a token force, contract labour being the order of the day. Thus the island has lost its main source of employment.

All this contributes to a breakdown of community spirit. In the housing sector, the policy of the early years was to control the letting to ensure a balanced population. All this is fast disappearing and the island's housing stock has become prey to market forces for, when a property becomes vacant, mainland rents are imposed, which has meant that some of the islanders have left the island. Now the number of true islanders has been reduced to near single figures.

Like many of the villages on the mainland, with the influx of 'outsiders', the local dialect is slowly fading, a dialect so distinguishable from the island's nearest neighbours in Burnham on Crouch and Great Wakering, commonly known to the Foulnessians as Blairum.

The locals still struggle to maintain village life. They still hold mini-Church fêtes and annual shows, when the defence authorities agree to 'open the gates' to all and sundry. Whist drives are still held in the village hall, where the ladies also enjoy carpet bowls, but no active sports are played on the island now, because there are insufficient residents to raise a team, although one side does play as Foulness Cricket Club — on the mainland.

Alas, Taylor's Dream is fast becoming a nightmare, for his proud boast in 1992 that newspaper had at last arrived on the day they were published, has all but turned full circle. No organised delivery exists, for a dwindling population has made it a non-viable venture. This has also been the fate of several ventures which came to the island in the 1920s.

What of the future? With the run-down of military needs, the island is virtually in limbo, the villagers struggle to survive against the odds, but Foulness has lost its charm of yesteryear and few would wish to forecast the future. That rests with Whitehall, which surely had plans for the island's future when building a six-million pound bridge to replace the Scherzer Rolling Life Bridge in 1988.

Time will tell. Who knows? It might even return to the private sector.

Postscript 2005 At last reprint with all receipts going to the Heritage Centre.

But without the sponsorship from the Heritage Trust and help and generosity of the Publisher who waived reproduction rights, it would not have been possible.

The Heritage Centre opened in 2003 and has been a great success, a welcome relief, as the island's population has lost amenities which mainland Britain takes for granted.

John S Dobson.

The FCAS would like to thank John Dobson for allowing and arranging the reproduction of "Foulness The Mystery Isle" so donating the proceeds by sale to the Heritage Centre.

The Foulness Home Guard.

114

ABOVE: Aerial view of the 1953 floods. (Purchased from the now defunct *News Chronicle* 1953.) OPPOSITE: Maplin Sands — The airport that never was. BELOW: Foulness Church, showing the wooden mortuary near the west gate, still the focus of local endeavour.

INDEX

ENDPAPERS: 1920 Ordnance Survey map.

SUBSCRIBERS

Presentation copies

1 Foulness Parish Council
2 Rochford District Council
3 Essex County Council
4 Southend Record Office
5 Foulness Archaeological Society
6 Shoeburyness Museum
7 Burnham Museum
8 Jim Worsdale

9 John & Vi Dobson
10 Clive & Carolyn Birch
11 Mr & Mrs D. Thorn
12-
13 R.H. Coleman
14 Raymond Vernon Wright
15 A. Ringwood
16 Laurie Young
17 Gwendolin May Thorn
18 Terry Dean
19 Mrs Pauline Dean
20 Miss Sarah Dean
21 Simon Dean
22 W.H.A. Smallwood
23 R.S.G. Wooding
24 Pat Thorn
25 Roger Harris
26 The Snewins (Australia)
27 S.M. Brown
28 Jim Worsdale
29 Paul Worsdale (USA)
30 G.M. Price, Ack Ack
   Foulness
31 Mrs Hawes
32 G.A. Dean
33 Mrs Murray
34 M. Astor
35 Betty Ward, A.A.BTY
   RA 1945
36 Elsie Williams
37 M. & S. Williams
38 H. & A. Potter
39 G. & K. Hubbard
40 J.I. Hume
41 Miss G.M. Kennard
42 John C. Monk
43 Mr Marsh
44 Peter Mead
45 Betty A. Allen
46 Mrs Ann Hardstaff
47 Mrs B. Yeo
48 J. Willsmer BEM
49 Graham Willsmer
50 M.G. Willsmer

51 C.J. Willsmer
52-
53 P.L. Carr
54 T.J. Gilmour
55-
56 M. Shelley
57 D. Holmes
58 F.G.T. Farenden
59 Mrs B. Ferris
60 Major A.S. Hill (Retd)
61 R. Steward
62 Chris Hill
63 S.J. Dyer
64 Derek Hester
65 B. Sullivan
66 Kenneth Rochester
67 Mrs Nellie Pyall
68 Mrs V.M. Ball
69 Maureen Pavelin
70 Jean Wood
71 Margaret Tillbrook
72 Mrs A. Willoughby
73 D.J. Fitz-Gibbon
74 Mrs J. Threadgold
75 J.G. Evett
76 Beryl Mead
77 Mrs M. Boreham
78 Malcolm Igglesden
79 Mrs Aubrey Barrett
80 Steve Hume
81 Alan Dobson
82 E.C. Tillbrook
83 Linda Dobson
84 M. Smith
85 James Keith Dixon
86 Colin Self
87 R.J. Evans
88 Chris Johns
89 Mike Peer
90 E. Golden
91 Myra Kemp
92 J. North
93 Neil Thumpston
94 Lilian Blunt

95 Thomas Illman
96 J.R. Willsmer
97-
98 Mollie Drake
99 Peter Jeffries
100 M.J. Wolstencroft
101 G. Wiseman
102 Kevin Mint
103 Mrs A.B. Elliot
104 R. Pearson
105 P.W. Mead
106-
109 Dr S.H. Dobson
110 B.N. Targett
111-
113 Mrs L.R. Farr
114-
115 J.L. Belton
116 C.R. Cripps
117-
118 B.M. Dent
119 Robin Sunderland
120-
121 Mrs G. Beale
122 Stephen Pewsey
123 Philip Pewsey
124 Bob Cole
125 Brian Shannon
126 Mrs J.A. Brown
127-
128 R.D. Rawlings
129 Terry & Gay Gorton
130 Mrs Donaldson
131 Kenneth Ross Seath
132-
133 Susan Tillson
134 Mark King
135 D.E. Everett
136 John Frederick Cottis
137 Mrs M. Hyam
138 Doreen Grant
139 R. Wood
140 R. Robinson
141 R. Barttram

142 Jean Mason	206 Brian Martin	271 Brian Weston
143 Nick Mason	207 G. Baron	272 Bill Walker
144 W. Burrows	208 Mrs E.E. Bradley	273 Lilley & Hume Families
145 E.G. Cripps	209 Eric J. Lucking	274 Stella Harrod
146 H. C. Bassingthwaighte	210 James Threadgold	275 Mrs G. Bolton
147 Joe Patience	211 T. Mann	276 Alan Dyer
148 Roy Ducker	212 A. Overall	277 Jan Thorpe
149 Stephen Ducker	213 V.A. Bland	278 J.F. Chapman
150 Miss V.M. Seadon	214-216 Mrs A. Boultwood	279 James Graham
151 Alec Willsmer		280 N.T. Sudell
152 Mr & Mrs F. Harris	217-219 Mrs F. Beckwith	281 G.S. Jones
153 R. Foster		282 Geoffrey Farrell
154 John Shelley	220 Mrs K. Cracknell	283 D.G. Eve
155 Cllr M.C. Brown (Rochford D.C.)	221 Mrs Ruby Havelin	284 Mrs Gwen Story
	222 Grace Nichols	285 A.G. Hunt
156 Malcolm Bullock	223 Percy Belton	286 P.W. Fisher
157 I.C. Leys	224-226 Cliff Hume	287 Margaret Crossman
158 Mrs Daisy Crabb		288 N.J. Gayner
159 P. Denny	227 Richard Sykes	289 G.D. Reeve
160 Michael Crabb	228-229 Mrs G. Hall	290 M. Ebsworth
161 P.A. Bridge		291 Mrs Ann Leonard
162 F.G. Nunn	230-231 S.P. Wisken	292 A.P. Quy
163 E.J. Everett		293 Dr D.I. Acres
164-165 H. Bird	232 Kathleen Mary White	294 Dennis Nisbit
	233 F.J. Thompson	295-310 Essex County Council
166 Lee Fox	234 Tony & Doreen Baker	
167 Muriel Sutherland	235 Raymond M. Palmer	311 Mrs Mary Allen
168 John Mead	236 P.J. Rolph	312 J.L. Lawrence
169 Sonny Perry	237 L.A. Lee	313 J.E. Joscelyn
170 John Edward Hooke	238 Maurice Adcock	314 James Mackie JP
171 K.W.J. Sanders	239 A.A. Flood	315 Miss B.M. Hardy
172 Peter Huxter	240 Dawn Bailey	316 John Massey
173 Mrs Jean Fraser	241 P. Ladbrook	317 Chelmsford Library
174 Janet Cutherbert	242 Graham J. Butler	318 Kathleen Coley
175 T.F. Childs	243 G.M. Rawlingson	319 Sylvia Schwinghammer
176-178 Mrs Ruth Briggs (née Hume)	244 A.H.W. Boniface	320 George R. Cooper
	245 Mr & Mrs A. Willsmer	321 Graham Wilkinson
179 W.J. Lilley	246 Helen Bushnell	322 L.B. Dobson
180 Miss C. Nichols	247 F.J. Thompson	323 R.M. Sayer
181 J. Harrod	248 T. Marshall	324 Geoffrey M.W. Mann
182 R. Henshaw	249 Andrew Lane	325 Dr Michael Clark MP
183-184 D. Tillbrook	250 David Lane	326-327 Jean Rogers
	251 Wendy Amery	
185 Mrs D.A. Chittock	252-253 Mrs C. Cornwall	328-329 A. Mead
186-189 Southend Library		
	254 R.W. Crump	330-332 I.C. Cooper
190 Anthony Potter	255 D.W. Ames	
191 Edward Parsons	256 K.D. Hatley	333-334 Mrs Tanner
192 Phil Adcock	257 Brian Ford	
193 Keith Angliss	258 Mrs C.D. Illman	335 Richard G. Rae
194 Hunt Roche	259 Mrs G. Beale	336 David R. Noble
195 Denis Coughlan	260 Chris Hebden	337 Mrs E.M. Patten
196-197 Judith M. Smith	261 Kevin Cummins	338 N. Slaymaker
	262 Don Hebden	339 John Townsend
198 R.J. Fairman	263 Richard Payne	340 Paul Watts
199 Rod Watson	264 Roy Muskett	341 T. Dean
200 Mark Rawlings	265 Madeline Barnes	342 Gordon Allen
201 The Thorpe Bay School	266 Dorothy Hone	343 Dr Peter Watson
202 Michael James Galley	267 D. Whitmore	344 George Henry Parker
203 Geoffrey C. Lee	268 Captain J.L. Haynes	345 G. Cane
204 Maurice F. Christophers	269-270 June Cork	346 Richard B. Collins
205 David A. Spencer		*Remaining names unlisted.*

120

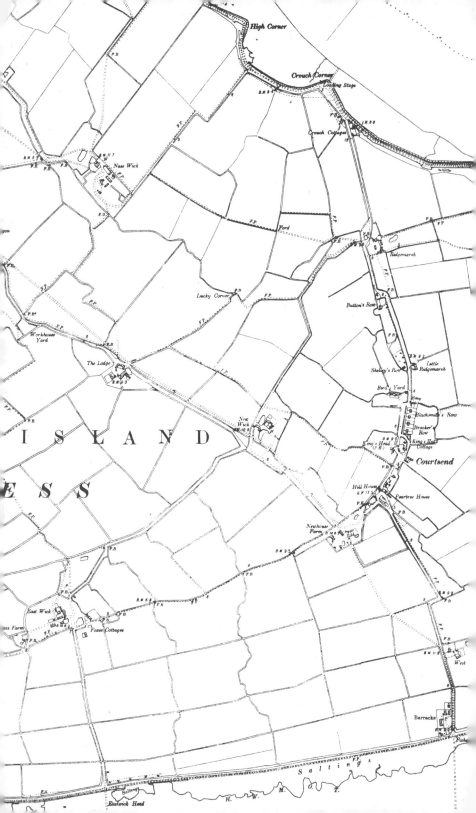